Crime,
class and
corruption

D1382370

Simon Stone

Bookmarks
London, Chicago and Melbourne

Crime, class and corruption: the politics of the police

Audrey Farrell

Crime, class and corruption: the politics of the police /
Audrey Farrell
First published July 1992
Second printing March 1993
Bookmarks, 265 Seven Sisters Road, London N4 2DE
Bookmarks, PO Box 16085, Chicago, Il. 60616
Bookmarks, GPO Box 1473N, Melbourne 3001
© Audrey Farrell and Bookmarks
ISBN 0 906224 70 5
Printed by Cox and Wyman Limited, Reading, England

Bookmarks is linked to an international grouping of socialist
organisations:
AUSTRALIA: **International Socialist Organisation**,
GPO Box 1473N, Melbourne 3001
BELGIUM: **Socialisme International**,
Rue Lovinfosse 60, 4030 Grevignée
BRITAIN: **Socialist Workers Party**,
PO Box 82, London E3 3LH
CANADA: **International Socialists**,
PO Box 339, Station E, Toronto, Ontario M6H 4E3
CYPRUS: **Workers Democracy**,
PO Box 7280, Nicosia, Cyprus
DENMARK: **Internationale Socialister**,
Ryesgade 8, 3, 8000, Århus C
FRANCE: **Socialisme International**,
BP 189, 75926 Paris, Cedex 19
GERMANY: **Sozialistische Arbeitersgruppe**,
Wolfsgangstrasse 81, W-6000, Frankfurt 1
GREECE: **Organosi Sosialistiki Epanastasi**,
PO Box 8161, 10010, Omonia, Athens
HOLLAND: **Groep Internationale Socialisten**,
PO Box 9720, 3506 GR Utrecht
IRELAND: **Socialist Workers Movement**,
PO Box 1648, Dublin 8
NORWAY: **Internasjonale Sosialister**,
Postboks 9226, Grønland 0134, Oslo
POLAND: **Solidarnosc Socjalistyczna**,
PO Box 12, 01-900 Warszawa 118
SOUTH AFRICA: **International Socialists of South Africa**,
PO Box 18530, Hillbrow 2038
UNITED STATES: **International Socialist Organisation**,
PO Box 16085, Chicago, Il. 60616

Contents

Tables and Figures

Tables

Figures

To Sally, Tom, Robert and Josie with love

Acknowledgements

I wish to thank Sally Kincaid for her patient work on the
graphics. Charlie Hore and Pete Alexander gave much help with
early rambling drafts as did Phil Taylor, Colin Barker and Derek
Howl. Duncan Hallas gave me gems of advice. Lindsey German,
Ian Taylor and, in particular, Duncan Blackie with great
pleasantness and tact turned the final
draft into a book.
For support, tolerance, encouragement and advice I thank the
comrades from Leeds West and Leeds East Socialist Workers
Party branches, trade union colleagues and students at work,
John and Sue Nightingale and family, Dennis Farrell,
Jim Kincaid, David Coates and Liam Duffy. Thanks also to
Alex Callinicos, who told me to start the book and to the Fryston
miners, the printworkers and the 'Sunday football crowd' who
inspired me to finish it.
Audrey Farrell, May 1992

Audrey Farrell is a member of
the Socialist Workers Party in Britain.

Introduction

THE LAST decade has shattered the myth that Britain has a uniquely benevolent police force. Crude corruption has been exposed in headline cases. Innocent Irish people—the Birmingham Six and the Guildford Four—were released years after being given life sentences for bombings they did not commit and could not have committed. Three young men were similarly fitted up after the death of a policeman during rioting on the Broadwater Farm estate in north London. All these cases showed the police were prepared to use terror tactics to obtain false confessions and frame the innocent in order to get results.

These were the big cases, but corruption was shown to run far wider. In 1989 the whole of the West Midlands Regional Crime Squad was suspended amidst a massive scandal.

Police violence was seen time and again on TV and experienced first hand by large numbers of people. Riot squads attacked miners in 1984-5; print workers in 1983 and 1986-7; the youth of the inner cities in 1981, 1985 and 1991; and, most disastrously for them, the 200,000 strong demonstration that assembled in London in March 1990 to kill off the poll tax and Margaret Thatcher's long reign.

Such events have put a decisive end to the period which followed the war in which it was easy to make the claim that the police were servants of the public, on hand to protect and help out. An increased number of people say they do not support the police, up from 10 percent in 1981 to 25 percent a decade later.[1]

Hatred of police action has spread far wider than the establishment would have liked it to. Resentment is no longer mainly restricted to black people, young people and the left. Large numbers of 'respectable' working class people have seen their attempts to save jobs and communities dealt with by the blows of a police truncheon.

Such is the crisis in confidence in the police that the most detailed independent study of the force ever undertaken concluded that greater contact with the public would only discredit them further.[2]

Nevertheless, the same statistics which show falling police credibility also show the vast majority of people still believe they perform a useful role.

As much as confidence in the police is shattered by their most notorious antics, a widescale fear of crime also generates the conviction that the police are needed to ensure public safety and defend people's property. True, the levels of particular types of crime in our society are systematically played up in the media and by the police themselves. Nevertheless, crime is still a real concern.

These two factors in tandem appear to make sense of the most common idea about what should be done to the police. Violence, corruption and racism should be dealt with in order that the police can more effectively get on with the business of solving crime. In other words, the police should be reformed.

But closer examination reveals holes in this argument. For one thing, the police are *astonishingly* bad at dealing with the crimes that affect ordinary people. London is the most intensively policed city in Britain, yet the police clear up less than 8 percent of burglaries. The figures for the rest of Britain are also extremely low.[3]

Are the British police just a dozy collection of individuals? Could they improve their record if they concentrated more on crime and less on harassing people? Will community policing give us the kind of force that existed in the legends of the 1950s?

The argument of this book is that the problem lies much deeper than this. The police are useless at dealing with crime because of the very nature of the institution and the society in which they work. Our argument is that crime is generated by capitalism.

A system based on inequality, greed, wealth and need is bound to create the conditions in which some people at least find they have to steal in order to get by. A system which cramps people in inadequate, overcrowded housing and encourages people at every turn to look out only for themselves is bound to push some people into using violence against others.

Even London's Deputy Chief Constable conceded in 1992 that social deprivation creates crime. Here lies the first problem: the task the police are supposed to deal with—stopping crime— has roots in a much broader set up over which they have no control.

More than this, not only are the police incapable of dealing with the crimes that affect ordinary people, they are not really concerned with them at all.

The mobilisations which were used against the miners and poll tax demonstrators were not aberrations—they are the historical rule. The modern police force originated in an attempt by a frightened ruling class to deal with the great urban concentrations of people that developed with capitalism itself. Every great upsurge of struggle has been met with police attacks and been followed by an increase in police numbers. This was true of the Chartist struggles in the middle of the last century and the Great Unrest which preceded the First World War. It was true of the 1926 General Strike and the battles during the crisis-torn 1970s and 1980s.

'Property is nine tenths of the law', as the saying goes. It is correct, but not specific enough. The police's job is to protect in particular the property of the rich and powerful. If the ruling class's extravagant personal belongings are threatened by individuals who have little, then the police are on hand to make sure that wealth stays with the wealthy. If the flow of their profits is disturbed by strikes, then the police are available to keep the factory gates open. If the existence of their privileged position at the top of society is challenged, then the police can be called on to defend it.

The police therefore have the job of defending the very system that generates crime. Little wonder they can do little to stop it.

This book starts with a detailed examination of the myths that surround police work and shows why it is that they fail to protect ordinary people, while turning a blind eye to the crimes of the rich and powerful. It then goes on to chart the development of the modern force as a response to class struggle.

Other issues make sense once we understand the police as

servants of the ruling class rather than as servants of us all. It is possible to develop an understanding of the social position of the ordinary police officer. Is he or she an ordinary employee, like those with similar pay and control over their work? Or does the police officer's position and day to day experience invalidate the claim that they are simply 'workers in uniform'?

Why are the police so racist—with Black people they charge three and a half times more likely to be detained than White people—and could they be made less so through better training or an increase in the number of Black officers? Why is it that the police deal with football crowds as if it were an exercise in social containment rather than a matter of public safety?

Finally, we will look at a real solution to crime, which starts by understanding its roots and the need to fight for a different kind of society from the one which the police defend and which presently generates horrors at every turn.

Chapter one

Violence and society

'TO PREVENT and detect crime, to protect life and property and to preserve the Queen's Peace'.[1] This is the official police role. Even people critical and suspicious of the police measure their performance against these criteria. But are the police really meant to provide such protection?

Even the most cursory glance says not. Great swathes of social violence are untouched by the police. They do not prevent toxic pollution, transport disasters or industrial deaths. Nor do they campaign against the violence of health and welfare cuts. Much of society's violence is not even defined as crime.

How far do the police prevent the interpersonal violence that is seen as their area of concern? Can the police protect us by preventing the most extreme form of personal violence—murder? If we look at the nature of the offence and the likely circumstances of its occurrence, we can see that the police play a minimal role in its prevention.

The incidence of murder, particularly those carried out by complete strangers, is greatly exaggerated in the media and police mythology. In England and Wales in 1988 there were only 103 convictions for murder, 168 for manslaughter and 6 for infanticide (with 221 court decisions pending). That made a total of 592 offences recorded as homicide.[2] This is a small number compared with a population of 52 million. (There were a further 339 offences of causing death by reckless driving.)[3]

As can be seen from Figure 1 on page 14, in 65 percent of homicide cases the victim and principal suspect were either members of the same family, lovers or friends. In only 26 percent of cases were victims and chief suspects strangers. In the case of women victims the proportion was even lower at 13 percent. Nor is it true that all these strangers leapt out at their victims in a completely random and unpredictable manner. According to an official survey:

The relationship between victim and principal suspect is not always recorded and so the 'other stranger' category may include some victims who were in fact known to, or related to, the principal suspect. By far the largest group (65 persons; 45 percent) of persons killed by apparent strangers

Figure 1. Offences recorded as homicide by relation of victim to chief suspect.[4]

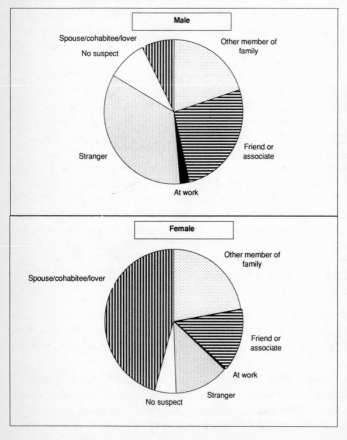

were killed as a result of an argument; about half of these arguments took place in or outside a public house or other place of entertainment.[5]

The incidence of violence in the street has been greatly exaggerated by the police in order to justify their role and presence there. By contrast, they also have an interest in down-playing the threat in one of the real battlegrounds of our society—the home.

Domestic violence has a low priority in policing, despite its frequency. The nuclear family in modern capitalist society reproduces, nurtures and controls the future labour force. Part of the police's function is to defend the institution of the family which often means sacrificing the well-being of the women and children. The family, while a 'haven in a heartless world' can often also be a violent place, a cauldron where personal relationships boil over into aggression.

The police have been reluctant to intervene in fights between married people, even since the 1976 Domestic Violence and Matrimonial Proceedings Act. The authoritative Policy Studies Institute report found that, 'the clearest example of what PC's called "rubbish" are domestic disputes and disturbances.'[6] An unpublished Metropolitan Police report into domestic violence carried out by a team of police officers and social workers condemned the police for failing to take wife battering seriously. The inquiry team found that police methods of documenting cases of wife battery disguised the extent of the problem and treated domestic violence as a second class matter. The police were, 'Fully aware of their right to charge, but tended to leave this option for cases where death was imminent or likely.'[7] The seriousness of domestic violence is known and yet the 1986 Metropolitan Police report voiced fears that police,

> involvement in cases of matrimonial violence could affect their promotion prospects... [and that they also] felt unable to use police vehicles to remove women to refuges because of mileage allowance rules.[8]

More recently, a cosmetic change has been forced on the official police view about domestic violence. The Metropolitan Police Commissioner's Report for 1989 boasted that more incidents of domestic violence were being recorded rather than being 'no crimed', taking the police statistics on domestic violence an inch nearer to reality. But changing police statistics does not solve the problem. Nor can domestic violence be stopped by an increase in police intervention. That intervention will invariably be after the event. Problems with economic, social or psychological origins can't be solved by a dose of outside force. Escape from violent relationships requires financial provision, alternative accommodation and child care. The state is willing to provide none of these.

Family violence isn't limited to wife battering. Adolescents attack parents, men and women violently abuse children. The family itself, with its claustrophobic love-hate relationships, imprisons young and old in impossible proximity. The privacy of the family provides its sanctuary but also preserves its violence. It wasn't until 1889 that cruelty to a child by its parents became a criminal offence, so important was it to capitalism that parents should control and discipline their children.

Myth and reality

EXAGGERATING the dangers outside the home and minimising the dangers inside it reinforces the idea that a strong body of police are needed on the streets. Sixty percent of old women are frightened to go out at night because of the fear of violent assault. Senior police officers sometimes talk of, 'no go areas in city suburbs for the elderly'.

But the elderly and defenceless are not the typical victims of violence. In 1986 old people constituted only 3 percent of violent offence victims.[9] The odds on being assaulted were much higher for those who were male, under 30 years old, single, widowed or divorced; and those who spent several nights a week out, drank heavily and assaulted others. Research at Bristol Royal Infirmary casualty department in 1988 revealed that,

> four out of five serious assaults are never reported to the police... In the six months of the survey not one of their patients was elderly... Most were young working class men... the majority were aged between 15 and 25 and were involved in fights outside pubs. The average male victim had knocked

back the equivalent of five and a half pints of beer before being beaten up.[10]

Why then the media emphasis on attacks on the old? Of course attacks on old people are horrific. But why increase the fears of the old to venture out or even to answer the door? The point of exaggerating the vulnerability of the old and weak is to justify demands for a strong and numerous police force.

The violence associated with property offences is also hyped up to create a general atmosphere of fear and the need for police protection. Although burglary and robbery are considerably under-reported, these are essentially offences against property rather than against the person.

The police have no role in preventing interpersonal violence at work. This usually takes the form of frustrated outbursts against workers in understaffed institutions from those suffering welfare, health or housing cuts. Young underpaid nurses are particularly at risk in understaffed, ill-equipped hospitals, with 38 percent of student nurses reporting injuries from patients.[11]

In children's homes and hostels for young people, or in old people's homes it is the thousands of day to day carers who face the possibility of violent assault as an occupational hazard.[12] As public transport is cut back and bus drivers do two jobs and face public frustration at inadequate services they too have to deal with violence from or between passengers. Unions force employers to take protective measures; not the police. In Strathclyde in 1985 the Social Work Department of the Regional Council had to strike in order to get 'official recognition that staff were the victims of violence as part of their normal working life'.[13]

So much of the violence in society is the product of stress arising from poverty, frustration, overcrowding, or illness. Therefore, social violence, by its very nature, affords little preventative role to the police. Even when the police do restrain someone who is behaving aggressively or place them under arrest, the violent offender does not stop being violent simply because they are imprisoned in institutions where violence, terror and degradation are the normal forms of control. Prisoners are attacked by prison officers and other prisoners. Although the terror is locked away from public view, that doesn't mean society's violence has been reduced.

In some incidents the police delay their response or appear on the scene to arrest or attack the victims rather than the assailants. This is particularly true of racist attacks.

A Home Office study in 1981 on racial attacks indicated that an Asian person was 50 times more times likely to be the victim of racially motivated incidents than Whites.[14] This report produced a conservative estimate of 7,000 attacks a year but another study, by the Policy Studies Institute, concluded that the real total—of recorded and unrecorded cases—could be ten times higher.[15]

A report produced by the Institute of Race Relations criticised the way police played down racial attacks—sometimes redefining the problem so that for example, 'Racial harassment becomes a dispute between neighbours. They were able to cite examples where the victims were arrested, rather than the attackers.'[16] The report further stated:

> Despite claims by senior officers that policing racist attacks is a major priority, the attitude ordinary officers display is that racist attacks are not a policing concern.[17]

This problem does not just arise from the racism of individual constables. A 1989 government report on Racial Attacks stated:

> In the course of our investigation we have noted an apparent belief among some police officers that they will be 'marked down' by their senior officers if they acknowledge that racial incidents are occurring on their patch.[18]

Another major category of interpersonal violence after family and racial attacks is violence between drinking acquaintances. It is usually bar staff and the combatants' friends that prevent or cool out pub fights, often before injuries become serious. According to a Home Office study, between 1950 and 1988 growth in beer consumption was the 'single most important factor in explaining the growth in violence against the person'.[19]

A new moral panic was blown up by police and media in 1988: 'rural riots'; fights in country towns between mainly employed 'lager louts'. The new panic was used to claim that social deprivation had nothing to do with crime. But fights at closing time even in country areas have a longer history than the police themselves. At the time of the introduction of the rural police in the mid nineteenth century a magistrate said optimistically that before,

> the establishment of the rural police (drinking and rowdyism were winked at) but in future they would be prevented.[20]

Sending in a heavy mob does not stop violence amongst groups of youths. The police in this situation are 'just another firm' of louts with uniforms and truncheons liable to do more physical damage. Take this pertinent observation made by the Chief Constable of the Thames Valley force which officially topped the league for violent disturbances in 1988. He said most 'rural' disturbances,

> begin with a minor incident *that escalates once the police arrive on the scene*. There are times when we are slow to respond and it doesn't become such a serious incident.[21]

Whilst people who have been drinking do commit violent offences, those who are arrested for being drunk and incapable are at risk of very severe violence or medical neglect at the hands of the police.

Who's killing whom?

THE NUMBER of deaths caused directly by the police is difficult to establish. Inquest, an organisation formed in 1980 by friends and families of people who had died at police hands estimated that between 1970 and 1985 over 300 people had died in London either in police custody or as a result of other police activities.[22]

In 1989 there were 37 deaths in police custody in the Metropolitan Police area.[23] Only 3 out of 17 coroners' inquests into such cases in 1989 found verdicts of 'natural causes'. There were 2,372 complaints of assault carried out by the London police in 1989.[24] But there is little hope of redress from the police complaints system where the initial investigations are carried out by the local police force themselves. For example in 1988, of 21,825 complaints made against the police outside the Metropolitan area, criminal proceedings against the police were taken in only 21 cases.[25] Complainants are often threatened with being charged with wasting police time. Registering a formal complaint and getting an investigation underway is a lengthy and nerve racking process.

There are no clear statistics about what actually occurs in police and prison cells. However, we do get some glimpse of police violence from these complaints figures and from the most public incidents—police shootings.

Among the most famous cases are the police shooting of five-year-old John Shorthouse in 1985 and the pregnant young woman Gail Kinchin in a siege in 1983; of Steven Waldorf shot 'by mistake' in Central London in 1984 and of Cherry Groce during a house raid in 1985. There was an escalation in the issue of guns to the Metropolitan Police in the 1970s which bore no relationship to any increase in armed crime. While the number of armed crimes roughly doubled through the 1970s, the issue of police firearms went up over four times.[26]

There was a move in the mid 1980s to create a smaller, but more highly trained pool of police who would be issued firearms. But this did not increase the safety of the public. In August 1990 psychiatric patient Ian Gordon was shot dead by police. He was carrying an air pistol which could not be fired. In 1991 another man was shot dead in West Yorkshire by police during a siege in which he had only replica weapons.

When the police are called on very rare occasions to deal with deranged people with guns they are in fact completely ineffective. Sixteen people were killed by a berserk gunman in Hungerford before the police did anything. Indeed their major contribution was to delay ambulances getting to seriously injured victims.[27]

One attempted justification for the arming of the police is the claim that they are in a very dangerous position. In truth the police are more likely to be the perpetrators of violence than its victims. In terms of fatalities at work, policing is one of the safer occupations. The figures for police and prison officers' deaths are often quoted together in official statistics, presumably because police deaths are so few. In the ten years to 1987, 22 police officers were killed. Even if police officers killed in road accidents are added to the total, policing is still one of the safest jobs, as can be seen from Table 1.

There was a time when official statistics were published which revealed that more London police officers were injured on

Table 1. Fatal injuries at work, 1987-8[28]

Industry	Number
Construction	158
Agriculture and forestry	63
Merchant seafaring and fishing	60
Transport and communication	54
Mineral extraction, chemical manufacture	43
Distribution, hotels and catering	41
Metal goods, engineering and vehicles	36
Police and Prison Officers	11*
Insurance, Banking and Finance	6
*including 8 police killed in road accidents	

the field of sport than in the line of duty.[29]

If the police did protect us from violence, then it might be argued that a certain amount of police violence was justified. However, there is no evidence that the police play any but a residual role in stopping violence. There is certainly no evidence that they are able to protect us from interpersonal violence because of the very circumstances of its occurrence.

What about the police role in dealing with the most common cause of injury and death: the road vehicle? In 1988 63,400 serious injuries and 5,050 deaths in road accidents were reported, almost ten times the homicide figure.[30] Traffic control, road crossing patrols, vehicle checks, safety advice, training schemes for young cyclists and motor cyclists and campaigns against drink driving could all be socially useful and protective. But many of these functions are gradually being done by traffic wardens and civilians. In 1983 only 4 percent of the total strength of the Metropolitan Police was employed in the traffic division.[31] Accident prevention is just not a priority. Sir Kenneth Newman, then Commissioner of the Metropolitan Police, admitted as much in 1983 when he indicated that the time had come to stop pretending the police could address all problems with the same level of competence. Priorities had to be established. Not every traffic blackspot could be policed.[32]

The Metropolitan Police has consistently failed to even staff school crossings where necessary.[33]Meanwhile, it makes a grim contribution itself to the mayhem on the roads. Police cars in London alone were involved in accidents at the rate of 2,000 to 3,000 a year in the 1970s.[34] After the 1984 Road Traffic Regulation Act waived speed limits for emergency vehicles the police car accident rate moved up to over 4,000 a year in the 1980s and in 1988 they were involved in 5,400 accidents.[35] In London the accident rate involving personal injury with police cars is two and a half times that of taxi cabs. The inability of the police to enhance road safety is a function of their perceived role in crime prevention. As the Policy Study Institute report **The Police in Action** states, police car chases relieve boredom and 'offer a kind of excitement that police officers particularly hanker after'.[36] This finding is reiterated by Inquest's **Death in the City**:

> A key ingredient in modern police culture is the car chase... The usual impulse which leads to cars racing through built up areas at speeds of up to 100 mph is not aggression but boredom. The car chase is one of the rare opportunities for mobile patrols to feel that they are seriously involved in maintaining law and order.[37]

Can it be argued that speeding to the scene of the crime is an important aspect of crime prevention? Not according to Home Office research:

> It is now recognised that the advantages of fast response are less than had been previously supposed... in most major cities the police can get to the scene of a crime within minutes... a large American study found that no more than 3 percent of crimes reported to the police resulted in arrests which could be attributed to the speed with which a patrol reached the scene of the crime... Where offenders are disturbed in the course of crime, they can make good their escape... in seconds rather than minutes. But for most crime... The first reaction of victims is not to call the police, but... perhaps, to seek advice, reassurance or help from friends and neighbours ... crimes are not reported at the first opportunity but only after some delay, almost invariably more than ten minutes and often as long as three quarters of an hour.[38]

Speeding police cars have a negligible effect on crime prevention. The sound of a police siren or the sight of a flashing blue light certainly does not make people feel a sense of increased personal safety on the roads. The police play no role in stopping the violence of big business and their lives are not in continual danger.

These basic myths of police work shattered, let's now look more closely at their overall relevance to dealing with crime.

Chapter two

Crime: fact and fiction

WHAT DO the police actually do? The most common myth is that they spend their time 'catching crooks' and therefore protecting most members of society. But do they? Examine first the myth that the police protect *our* property.

There are many laws which aim at protecting property in general. Nominally *all* homes are protected by law. For many the home, for all its claustrophobia and potential violence, is the only place where time does not belong to the employer. Although, particularly for women, it may also be a prison, that does not make its violation any less upsetting. In the vast majority of cases burglary victims don't have expensive possessions. In 64 percent of the burglaries recorded in 1988 the value of the property stolen was under £500. In only 2 percent of burglaries were the goods worth more than £5,000.[1]

Yet burglary—one of the most upsetting crimes for working class families—is not a police priority. Between 1983 and 1989 there was an official policy of screening off crimes not likely to be solved.[2] This was concentrated on burglaries, an admission that this is a type of crime about which the police can do little. As a Home Office research report pointed out:

An average foot beat in a large British city covers a square half mile with 4.5 miles of public roadway and a population of about 4,000. Thus, given the present burglary rates and evenly distributed patrol coverage, a patrolling policeman in London could expect to pass within 100 yards of a burglary in progress roughly once every eight years, but not nec- essarily to catch the burglar or even realise that the crime was taking place.[3]

Former Metropolitan Police Commissioner Robert Mark told

a security conference in 1979 that,

> the belief that the state can, or even wishes to, protect people
> effectively from burglary, breaking offences and theft should
> be abandoned, at least in the great cities, where inadequate
> numbers of police have other and much more demanding
> priorities. We have lived for too long in a world of pretence
> for which the entertainment industry is partly responsible.[4]

The inability of the police to prevent burglary has
encouraged the rise of security firms offering every form of
sophisticated anti theft device.[5] This is despite evidence that the
most effective deterrant to a burglar is the belief that a house is
occupied.[6] The burglary prevention industry, selling mainly to
those least vulnerable, does however create work for the police.
Many devices seem to be activated by the neighbour's cat. During
1986 the Metropolitan Police dealt with 258,296 automatic alarm
calls of which 252,780, or 98 percent, were false alarms.[7] It is
estimated that £33 million is spent each year by the police in
answering such false alarms.

From one block of London flats it was reported in May 1988
that 'Kensington police station has been receiving 999 calls from
them at a rate of one a week'.[8] The flats had been experiencing
every type of burglary from minor thefts to entire flat clearances.
The flats were police married quarters and looked after by the
Civilian Property Services Division of the Metropolitan Police![9]

This is just one crass example of the police's inability to
prevent crimes such as burglary which are 'opportunistic' as they
occur in a relatively random and unplanned fashion. Another
opportunistic crime, street robbery, cannot be prevented by the
police. The Home Office report, **Crime and Police Effectiveness** points out that,

> Intensive patrols only provide intermittent cover of large
> areas. Thus in the supposedly crime ridden streets of
> American cities, it has been estimated that a patrol officer
> will encounter a street robbery only once every 14 years.[10]

The same report also stated:

> There is little evidence that increasing the number or
> frequency of foot patrols actually reduces crime—although
> this may achieve other important objectives in terms of

public satisfaction and feelings of security... In this study [done in New Jersey] the introduction of foot patrols was greatly appreciated by residents and seemed to reduce fear of crime; but the researchers found no measurable impact on crime levels themselves—whether measured by police statistics or by victim surveys.[11]

For most people, getting back their property is more important than punishing the offender. But there is only one area of property theft where the police can claim any sort of success: stolen cars, 66 percent of which are recovered. But even the Police National Computer isn't much help in catching car thieves as nationally only 28 percent of such crimes were cleared up in 1988. In the Metropolitan Police area during 1989 the figure was just 10.9 percent.

When it is remembered that these are crimes recorded by the police and that the British Crime Survey suggests there are probably 'Twice as many domestic burglaries as are recorded... five times as many... robberies and eight times as many thefts from the persons as recorded', then the amount of property recovered becomes almost laughable.

Clear up rates vary, particularly between London and the rest of the country. In 1989 a clear up rate of 7.6 percent was

Table 2. Recorded Theft, Burglary, Robbery, 1988: Property recovered and clear up rate[12]

	Total property stolen (x£1,000)	Property recovered (x£1,000)	% of value recovered
Burglary	253,454	10,192	4
Robbery	35,952	5,035	14
Theft from the person	3,891	217	6
Theft or unauthorised taking of motor vehicle	722,241	475,402	66

given for recorded burglaries in London.[13] Outside London, the police claimed, as they do practically every year, a clear up rate of 33 percent.[14]

Even these dismal figures are overestimates as many burglaries are not reported. Surveys have been done which attempt to measure hidden crime. Both the General Household Survey and the British Crime Survey—which involve random samples of people being asked questions, rather than relying on reports to police—give some measure of unrecorded crimes. If we look at clear up rates relative to these estimates, then the police impact in clearing up property crimes is very small indeed. It is possible, for example, to estimate from these figures a clear up rate for 'theft from the person' of 1.5 percent.

The clear up rate is further exaggerated because it includes a number of property offences which convicted burglars ask to be 'taken into account', even though they may not have committed them. For example, the whistle was blown on Kent detectives by a serving officer who produced a report showing that between 1978 and 1979 the 'clear up' rate improved dramatically from 24.4 percent to 69.5 percent because the police extracted more confessions from convicted burglars, some of which were shown to be false.[15] More recently in Essex, Anthony Everett,

a man suffering from severe mental illness was interrogated in a police station for nearly three weeks until he confessed

Table 3. Offences and clear ups, England and Wales 1987.[16]

	No. of offences recorded by police	% of recorded crime cleared up	No. recorded offences cleared up	British Crime Survey estimate of offences	% clear up of all probable offences
Burglary	483,000	27	130,410	1,118,000	11
Robbery	30,000	21	6,300	177,000	4
Criminal damage	305,000	23	70,150	2,931,000	2

to 391 burglaries and thefts—many of which had been committed while he was in prison for earlier offences.[17]

It is not a particularly modern phenomenon to swell the clear up figures with crimes 'taken into account'. In 1943 a Clerk of the Court explained that, 'criminals are generally willing to admit other cases put to them by the police, so that they have nothing to fear in the way of further charges when they come out of imprisonment'.[18]

The police claim more success in catching violent offenders. The Metropolitan Police clear up rate for violence against the person in 1989 was given as 59 percent and for sexual offences as 51 percent.[19] However, this is due to the fact that in the majority of such cases the victim and offender are known to each other. It doesn't take a great deal of detective skill to find the identity of a wife batterer. As David Steer, tutor at the Bramshill Police College pointed out, it is usually the case that,

> three quarters of suspects caught carrying out the crime were still at the scene when the police arrived, and were known from the outset, or were among a small number of people who had the opportunity to commit the crime.[20]

Where crimes are committed by strangers in private or in a public place 'stealthily and quickly' no increase in police manpower is likely to reduce or improve detection rates. The hopelessness of the police in clearing up crimes against strangers was amply illustrated by the case of Peter Sutcliffe, the Yorkshire Ripper, who murdered 13 women before being caught. He was finally arrested by accident, not through scientific detection. The police interviewed Sutcliffe as a suspect ten times before his final accidental arrest.

Cooking the books

THE MYTH of detective work which has been passed down through fiction from Sherlock Holmes to Inspector Morse bears little relationship to the work of real detectives. Their ineffectiveness has led the Home Office itself to point out that the police have a very limited role in crime detection:

studies have shown that for the majority of crimes cleared up the offender's identity is plain from the outset; victims or witnesses can say who did it, or else the offender is caught red handed or clearly implicated in some other way.[21]

A comprehensive study of investigative work in the United States found,

> only about 3 percent of all index arrests appeared to result from special investigative efforts where organisation, training or skill could make any conceivable difference.[22]

If detectives don't 'solve crimes' what do they do? They spend a 'considerable proportion of their time in pubs',[23] 'officially' chatting to informers and getting information to make charges stick and often claiming overtime whilst drinking. Most detective work is concerned with preparing the case for the prosecution after an arrest, rather than discovering the identity of the offender.

Forensic laboratories are used to 'get convictions' rather than to discover the identity of offenders. The methods which the police use to get convictions are frightening. They are expected to get results and attempt to conceal their ineffectiveness by lying and constructing cases when under pressure. Many innocent people have gone to prison on the basis of pseudo-scientific evidence as the cases of the Guildford Four and the Birmingham Six clearly established.

The media presentation of crime tends to focus on those areas in which the clear up rate is reasonably high. Between 1955 and 1977 a quarter to a third of US peak TV time was devoted to law and order shows. Sixty percent of the fictionalised offences concerned murder, assault and robbery,[24] compared with just 6.8 percent in real life.[25] Similarly, newspaper editors can sell papers to bored readers by focussing on violent and dramatic crimes, but not by concentrating on the run-of-the-mill petty crimes which the police are useless at dealing with.

One of the greatest influences on recorded crime is the number of police who are looking for it. One study of evidence from places as far apart as Uganda and Tennessee links increases in crime figures to increases in the number of police.[26] In addition, local statistics in relation to specific crimes should be treated with some caution.[27] A sudden change might simply reflect a change in chief constable. For example:

> Mr James Anderton was appointed Chief Constable of
> Greater Manchester on July 1 1976. That year 55 search
> warrants were executed under the Obscene Publications Act
> and there were proceedings in 25 cases. The comparable
> figures in 1977 were 287 warrants and 134 proceedings.[28]

The inclusion of offences in one category rather than another
can also lead to an exaggeration of particular types of crime. For
example the British Crime Survey, which looked at victims'
reports, found that robberies rose by 9 percent between 1981 and
1987 compared with a 62 percent rise in robberies recorded by
the police.[29]

Distorted statistics can be used by the police in a particularly
vicious and racist way. For example, the Metropolitan Police produced figures showing a much greater increase in robberies in
Brixton than elsewhere in London between 1976 and 1980 which
they attributed to black youths. When analysed it was clear,

> that crimes such as pickpocketing, usually categorised as
> theft, were being defined in Brixton as violent offences.
> When the categories were combined, the figures for Brixton
> were similar to those for the Met. as a whole.[30]

Police figures are intermittently and deliberately leaked on
'mugging', an offence which does not even exist in law. The figures
are not based on court proceedings or arrests, but on police rec-
ordings of 'victim observations of the offender'. And,

> the effect of their loose use of the term is to attach sinister
> and violent associations to crimes which are not violent, and
> which do not necessarily involve great distress... It is
> common place for all thefts and robberies from the person to
> be referred to as 'muggings' and then for statistics on these
> crimes to be used to 'prove' the streets are unsafe.[31]

The most clearly established influence on the incidence of
real crime is the state of the economy. Unemployment and poverty drive greater numbers of people beyond the law in an
attempt to get by. But this causal link, the fact that most crimes
originate in the failings of capitalism, puts them well beyond the
influence of the police. As a police study, set up at the request of
the Metropolitan Police Commissioner, explained clearly:

the crime rate and the level of public tranquility are the consequences of a multitude of influences other than policing activity, and these other influences probably have far more importance than what the police do or don't do. To show that this is so, it is only necessary to point out that there have been societies without an organised police force but having a very low level of crime, and there are societies (such as the US at the present time) having highly developed and very expensive police forces, combined with a high level of crime.[32]

'Idle drones'

MODERN POLICE studies frankly admit that the police cannot effectively prevent crime and that increasing police numbers makes little difference to the real crime level.

But if they don't protect our persons and property what do all these police men and women actually do? We see them attending fires and accidents, but it's the firefighters and ambulance workers who do the dangerous and life saving work. Because of their very existence, the police are called upon to perform a number of useful service functions. Studies have shown that the majority of calls to police stations consist of matters such as cats stuck up trees, neighbours dumping rubbish over fences, domestic rows, stolen bicycles, lost children, people locked out of houses or cars, conveying urgent messages to relatives about accidents or deaths.

The police are often asked for simple information. But these service functions would be better performed by workers who saw them as socially useful tasks. The police regard such useful work as digressions from the high status function of crime fighting fictionalised on TV.

But police dramas miss out the most important aspect of the job. Most of the time police officers are bored out of their minds. They are looking for something to do, somebody to talk to or maybe push around. Somehow they have to get through the day and hopefully have something to report. As a report from the Policy Studies Institute said,

For a police officer, patrolling tends to be boring, not only because it's often uneventful, but also because it is rather aimless. A considerable amount of police behaviour can best be understood as a search for some interest, excitement or sensation. An officer on foot will often spend a whole shift without doing any police work, and without talking to anyone except to greet them and provide simple information. At night it is common for a 'walker' to spend a whole shift without talking to anyone at all. Even officers in cars with mainsets can spend several hours without responding to a call and without finding something to do on their own account.[33]

The earliest police were resented as 'unproductive parasites', 'idle drones ... lounging about our streets.'[34] The police are seen walking about, standing around, sitting in cars or vans, speeding dangerously with lights flashing. They are seen harassing young men, hot dog sellers and buskers. It is often assumed that they are doing something else. If a worker stands still he is seen to be resting or idling. If a policeman stands doing nothing he is seen to be carrying out the mystical and dangerous task of catching criminals and making society safer. This myth is obsessively reinforced by the media but is far removed from reality.

Chapter three

Class and corruption

MOST RECORDED crime is committed by the poor against the poor as any visit to a magistrates' court makes clear. The police only occasionally interfere in the crimes committed by the rich against the poor.

It has never been a police duty to protect workers from the violence of their bosses. The police may be brought to workplaces to investigate personal theft or theft from the employer but they don't come in to check that offences are not being committed under the Health and Safety Acts. This job has been left to a dwindling band of health and safety inspectors. Administrative measures rather than criminal action is taken against employers. Child employment law is continually broken under police eyes without action being taken.

The violence of employers in terms of industrial deaths, maiming and disease, are not, except in isolated incidents, the subjects of police concern. Where they are well organised, it is trade unions who provide workplace protection. The transport secretary was not arrested after a series of rail disasters in 1989; nor were the negligent owners of the death trap oil rig Piper Alpha. There was no immediate arrest of the owners of the *Herald of Free Enterprise*, the unsafe passenger ferry which sank with horrendous loss of life off Belgium. On the other hand, when seafarers struck in 1988 to try to defend safer staffing levels, the police protected the scab labour.

Many of the worst abuses against working people by those with economic power are not designated criminal. But even where particular actions of the rich are legally deemed crimes, the police are often kept out. We have seen the rigour with which they imposed the poll tax on ordinary people. By contrast, the

Inland Revenue manages to keep the majority of wealthy tax offenders completely away from the police. There are occasional exceptions such as the imprisonment of jockey Lester Piggott or the unsuccessful prosecution of Ken Dodd for tax offences. Where the criminal law is used it is often the most marginal employers who get the harshest treatment. Bankrupt small builders or lump labourers are the favourite targets for tax convictions. The multi millionaire Lord Vestey avoided paying millions in taxation and yet two building labourers on the lump were sent to prison for swindling the tax man out of £3,000.[1] The Inland Revenue normally adopts the position that if the offender cooperates, admits past misdeeds and agrees to a settlement, then the whole case will be conducted without any police interference. Over 100,000 cases a year result in financial settlement compared with under 200 criminal convictions.[2]

Large scale tax offences get little police attention but the police are likely to arrest social security offenders over very small sums. In 1983 there were 9,336 prosecutions in England and Wales for social security offences and 225 prosecutions for tax offences.[3]

The differential policy against poor claimants and often very rich tax offenders is clear: 'Inland revenue policy ... *should be that the criminal law is invoked as a last resort for "heinous" cases.*'[4] By contrast, for social security offences:

> The Departments... accept that in principle criminal prosecutions should take place in cases of abuse by wrongful claims whenever the evidence is reasonably adequate to secure a conviction, and that extenuating circumstances are a matter for the court rather than the prosecutor.[5]

It's difficult to get exact figures on the number of police officers hunting down tax evasion and company crime but in 1975 there were only, '35 police officers in the City of London and over 100 at Scotland Yard... engaged in the fight aganst white collar crime'[6], compared with the 2,488 DHSS special fraud *teams* operating in 1984.

The rich lay down conventions and rules for the conduct of their business. Occasionally the over-greedy, the careless or the failed may be handed over to the police. But the rich prefer to police their own.

In speculation on the stock markets, insider dealing is like a gambler playing with marked cards. It is not approved of within the ruling class, unless the successful gamblers are sharing their winnings. Insider dealing has now been made illegal but as Tory minister Cecil Parkinson made clear at the time: 'I do not expect to see hundreds of... highly respectable people being dragged before the courts.'[7]

The Inland Revenue dealt with tax fraud or evasion estimated in 1984 at £3 billion but neither they nor the Customs and Excise have any obligation to pass information on to the police.

The rich favour regulation by internal agencies such as the Securities and Investment Board. Yet the scale of the scandals at the self regulated Lloyds insurance market in the early 1980s made 'other city misdemeanours look trivial'.[8] Similarly, company investigations are carried out by the Companies Investigations Board of the Department of Trade and Industry. The Roskill Inquiry suggested the establishment of a Serious Fraud Office and the need for a unified organisation of Inland Revenue, Customs and Excise, the Department of Trade and Industry and the police.[9] But there was no suggestion that 'fraud' should be just a police concern.

This is no marginal field of crime. The Police Foundation found that fraud involving credit cards, cheques, expense frauds and embezzlement in London cost three times the total lost in house burglaries and car thefts.[10] One senior detective of the City Fraud Squad, Supterintendant Don Randall disclosed that,

> The City of London could point to £477m involved in cases of fraud or attempted fraud within the Square Mile in the year to July 1989... Fewer than a third of those interviewed said they reported all fraud to the police... In those companies admitting that employees were responsible 38 percent were found to be directors or managers.[11]

The police are called in by the government, through the Director of Public Prosecutions, to very few cases. But even when invited in, the police rarely take such crimes seriously. Sir John Wood, Principal Assistant of the Director of Public Prosecutions said,

> among the police there was a tendency to view fraud as a

Figure 2. City fraud cases

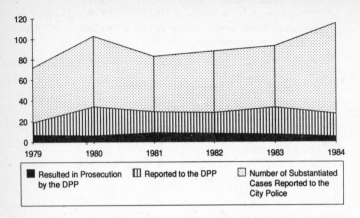

Legend:
- ■ Resulted in Prosecution by the DPP
- ▥ Reported to the DPP
- ▦ Number of Substantiated Cases Reported to the City Police

very low profile crime, and it was very difficult to persuade detectives that there was just as valuable a public service in sifting through the pages of a fraudulent company to obtain evidence of crime as there was in arresting a bank robber.[12]

The Director of Public Prosecutions also acts as yet one more filter to protect the rich from prosecution for fraud as Figure 2 shows.[13] The lack of police enthusiasm in dealing with high brow crime or what Al Capone called the 'legitimate rackets of the upper class' was well expressed by a City of London Chief Inspector:

> The police must be highly discreet and tread much more carefully than usual where crime in the business community is concerned. There are shareholders and policy holders to consider and police investigations could cause shares to fall and policy holders to panic. You can't go poking your nose into the affairs of the respectable and important companies without being extremely careful.[14]

Indeed, the dividing line between legal and illegal business is continually criss-crossed in the workings of the rich and powerful. Banks are anxious not to probe too deeply into the affairs of the rich, which is why the financial umbrella which protects tax evaders also extends to the proceeds of organised crime. Even so high a body as the New York Legislated Committee on Crime has recognised organised crime as simply an aspect of business:

> Organised crime is a continuing conspiracy to gain money and power without regard for law by utilizing economic and physical force, public and private corruption, *in an extension of the free enterprise system*.[15]

There is no way today in which the multi-billions made from narcotics can be realised without being laundered either through legal business concerns, fraudulent invoicing or the co-operation of banks and other financial institutions. Legal business concerns may be set up on the basis of illegal commodity market dealings and illegal operations may be started on the basis of money made in legal trading.

The same banks which protect tax evaders whose secrecy the ruling class want to preserve must also accept enormous cash deposits and withdrawals with no questions asked. Sometimes bizarre transactions leave bankers unruffled. After the £26 million Brinks Mat bullion robbery,

> Millions of pounds in £50 notes were taken from a local Barclays branch in carrier bags, cardboard boxes and paper sacks... a Bristol bank used to launder the money had to ask the Bank of England for extra £50 notes to keep up with the gang's withdrawals.[16]

Some of the Brinks Mat proceeds were used to buy a number of residential cottages belonging to Cheltenham Ladies College and, 'Cashing in on the London docklands property boom, they bought New Caledonian Wharf for £750,000 and sold it for £1.75 million.'[17]

Even the president of the FBI, William Webster, said, 'there are few businesses or industries in our community that are not affected by organised criminal enterprises.'[18]

Every now and then the ruling class sacrifices one of its own to pay a token tribute to the pretended classless nature of the law. Like a fruit machine, the state has occasionally to pay out to maintain its credibility. But when the police are allowed to nobble one rich crook a whole network of embarrassing relationships is often exposed. It is little wonder that where possible the rich keep the police out of their affairs.

Look at some of the relationships with top politicians and businessmen that have emerged in the publicised convictions of wealthy criminals. Lord Kagan, jailed for theft and fraud, has an interesting set of business associates including the late Sir Arthur Young, a former Commissioner of the City of London Police[19]; James MacDonald, Prince Phillip's senior valet; and Sir Rennie Maudsley who was responsible for the Queens' financial affairs.[20]

A similar embarrassing network of associates appeared in the Poulson case. John Poulson, once head of the largest architectural practice in Europe, was jailed in 1974 on corruption charges. Andrew Cunningham, who from 1964 to 1973 was chairman of the Durham Police Authority, was jailed at the same time. Reginald Maudling resigned as Home Secretary on account of his part in the scandal.[21] According to the Director of Public Prosecutions Reginald Maudling and others 'had received money from Poulson in connection with their services... what may have been improper... although it is not illegal... was that in promoting Poulson's interests in the House of Commons they failed to disclose their own financial involvement with Poulson'.[22]

Thus the idea that the police are permitted to pry into the rich business and criminal worlds at will is a myth. Often the Director of Public Prosecutions will step in to stop a case going to court if prosecution is not 'in the public interest' that is to say, not in the interests of the ruling class.

Those who make the big money in organised crime nest cosily within the protected ranks of big business. Nowhere is the hypocrisy sharper and the distinctions between business, crime and the police more blurred than in the world of drugs.

Drug squad

THE LAWS on drugs have little to do with the harmful or harmless nature of the drug in question. It is not criminal to produce or sell the dangerous, addictive drugs alcohol and tobacco but police are heavily involved in pursuing relatively harmless drugs such as cannabis.

All rational opinion testifies that cannabis is less harmful than either tobacco or alcohol, yet more police energy is spent on it than any other drug. Of the 10,471 offenders found guilty of

Table 4. Drugs and the police 1986.[23]

Drug	Number of cases dealt with
Cocaine	139
Heroin	1,357
LSD	229
Methadone	136
Cannabis	10,870
Amphetamines	2,011
Others	329

drug offences in 1986, 8,334 were done for alleged involvement with cannabis.[24]

The police have immense discretionary powers. This is because drugs serve different purposes in different times and contexts. The British ruling class which today rails against the 'evils' of the international trade, fought wars in the nineteenth century to open up China to the drugs trade for the East India Company. US president George Bush, who ordered the invasion of Panama in 1989 on the pretext of arresting its leader on drugs charges, was also instrumental in using drugs profits to fund US activities in Central America and the Middle East.

For the capitalists, drugs may impede workers' labour capacity but they are also a source of great profit and they can provide an individual escape for the worker which is less threatening to the boss than collective resistance.

Most workers have an ambivalent attitude towards illegal activities and commodities. Drugs may provide relief and excitement or be a source of livelihood for those involved in their production and distribution, but some drugs may also represent a real health threat. More importantly, ordinary people's *fears* of drugs can be turned to great advantage by the authorities.

Fear of drug addiction provides the justification for police harassment and interference, particularly in the lives of working class urban youth. Police credibility is reinforced by the idea that by waging a continual war against drugs they protect our children. However, the police war against drugs is more about repression and division than about social safety or well being.

The police role is not simply to curb the narcotics trade. The British police could not do this even if it were their main focus. The number of international and internal transactions are too great for police to monitor. Narcotics are small in bulk, easy to conceal and transfer. For example, 100,000 passengers may travel through Heathrow on a busy day and 500 ships may pass through Felixstowe in 3 months. A passenger ferry takes days to search; a cargo vessel weeks.

Because of these difficulties, the police's prefered tactic is to get involved with drug traffickers. But involvement in order to detect means the police themselves become part of the marketing process and are able to take their share of the profits. Even when a haul is made by the police and is destroyed, the only effect is to push up the street price and clear market space for other suppliers. In this way, the drugs trade mimics the behaviour of the production of any other commodity.

Britain has been a big market for cannabis since the 1960s onwards. The drug squad used undercover men and informants. In practice this meant,

> a system had to be created whereby certain dealers were in effect licensed by the Drug Squad to deal without much fear of prosecution. In return for providing a number of their customers as 'bodies' for the police, these favoured dealers could set up deals specially for the Drug Squad... The Home Office, once they discovered what was happening, had a name for this technique; they called it 're-cycling'.[25]

The drugs paid to informers were resold on the market. Sometimes police recycling was more direct. In 1976 publicity was given to a major police success in capturing 28 sackfuls of cannabis but these were lost on their way to destruction.[26] The following year another major police haul made in Essex was found to be adulterated with finger print powder.[27]

Such scandals crop up wherever there are police and drugs. In New York a third of the narcotics squad were indicted in 1974 after,

> 398 pounds of heroin mysteriously disappeared from the police property clerk's office, including the 70 pounds from the 'French Connection' case.[28]

Sometimes the police just pay informers to carry on trading, occasionally setting up a deal which will give the police a 'result'. The informers themselves may have been caught dealing. They may be bribed with the possibility of a letter to the judge stressing their co-operation and a promise of a short sentence or bail. The young dealer may be threatened with being stitched up if co-operation is refused. The effect is straightforward. There is no reduction of the trade. Some dealers operate with a police licence and others are arrested, but the trade continues.

Playing on workers' fears about the spread of drugs can be used to rationalise all sorts of racist, political or military manoeuvres. Curtailment of drug production may be used as an excuse for repression. For example, cocaine production has become central to the Bolivian economy since the collapse of the tin price. The British Home Office used the threat of cocaine imports as a reason for offering £600,000 to the Bolivian government for police training and equipment. Yet at the same time the British government claimed that, 'any international intervention to persuade the peasants to grow substitute crops was pointless'.[29]

Multinational narcotics are linked with secret police operations. The secret police in the Shah's Iran were connected with drugs. Iranian heroin came into Britain sometimes in legally protected diplomatic bags. Some of the Shah's own family had valuable monopolies in the opium trade.[30] The drug trade involves massive profits and violent competition. Like Chicago in the violent days of alcohol prohibition, the police share both the profits and the violence of the trade. Karl Marx explained this violence when he said a profit rate of,

> 10 percent will ensure its employment anywhere. 20 percent will produce eagerness; 50 percent positive audacity, 100 percent will make it ready to trample on all human laws; 300 percent, there is not a crime at which it will scruple, nor a risk it will not run.[31]

The rich in Britain are also involved with drugs. For example, Charles Tennant, the son of Lord Glencoma was fined £200 for trying to smuggle opium into the country. His mother was a lady in waiting to Princess Margaret.[32]

The death of Olivia Channon, daughter of the then Secretary of State for Trade and Industry, brought a number of wealthy users into the public eye. Sebastian Guinness, son of Jonathan Guinness; the Marquis of Blandford, heir to £50 million and great nephew of Winston Churchill; and Count Gottfried von Bismark all came before the courts in 1986 on offences related to heroin or cocaine.[33]

Ruling class efforts to protect their own young from heroin are hampered by their class's involvement in the lucrative trade. One gang caught attempting to smuggle £100 million of heroin into Heathrow included Anthony Hudson, the Old Etonian son of Sir Havelock Hudson, a former chairman of Lloyds.[34] In 1981 Martin Bendelow began a six year sentence for drug trafficking. He admitted importing cocaine worth several hundred thousands pounds:

> Few Conservative insiders doubted that Martin Bendelow was a rising star within the party. He was a close acquaintance of Sir Keith Joseph who became his political mentor and sponsored him as a parliamentary candidate.[35]

Needless to say, the police don't deal with these crimes by mass raids in Belgravia and Mayfair, as they would do on working class estates.

The 'war on drugs' is a class war, where the excuse of eliminating drugs is used as a means of terrorising working class youth. This was particularly the case with police raids on raves in the 1990s. In one such raid in Leeds in July 1990 the police moved in full riot gear on the youngsters' social event, blocking off the safety exits and making over 800 arrests. The main danger on that night was from the police, not drugs.

Narcotics are international big business. To produce any public 'results' in this international illegal commodity market with its own dynamic, super profits, multinational organisation and thousands of small producers and distributors, the police must enter the market either directly or indirectly. The media recognise in both fact and fiction that the police are involved in narcotics.

The pretence is that it is only a few bent coppers that dirty their hands. However corruption and police participation in competitive markets are not unfortunate deviations, they are inevitable police practices.

Bent coppers

THE ROTTENNESS is there to see: never a week goes by without some or other upholder of the public good being exposed for some racket. But are these rotten apples, degrading an otherwise healthy barrel?

Corruption in the sense of buying and selling favours, protecting the rich individually or brutalising prisoners to get confessions isn't incidental, it's central to policing. As we have seen, detection is largely fictional and therefore most 'results' in nailing criminals may come from accidents, confessions or fit-ups.

Rare accidents aside, there is no means of catching villains red handed unless the police know the time and place of a crime. To achieve this, one of the early advocates of preventive policing, Edwin Chadwick, emphasised the necessity of using informers and undercover police. He explained:

> The officers have been in the habit of employing thieves (who are called noses) to give them intelligence of the motions of their confederates. The nose is consequently tolerated in his own career. The chief distinction between the French and English system appears to be, that under the former, the noses have the name of *agents de police*, form part of the police establishments, and receive regular salaries.[36]

The use of informers is still central to policing. The greater the involvement of the informer in actually organising crime, the wider the information he is able to divulge and the more bodies are provided for police prosecution. It takes a *successful* thief to catch a thief. This type of relationship undermines the fraudulent notion that the police wage a relentless war against all law breakers.

It doesn't seem to matter that some informers may have long records of violent crime. Helping the police means that they can stay outside prison to carry on their careers for years. One such informer, Roy Garner, had committed arson, at least five armed robberies and had been found guilty of conspiring to pervert the course of justice in a murder trial. His rewards were considerable: allegedly £170,000 for information about one robbery, £37,000 for another. The BBC TV programme Brass Tacks was banned after producing an examination of the relationship between top criminals and the police, highlighting the activities of Garner.[37]

Police chiefs are socially linked with the business world of legal and illegal profit making. For example, John Dellow, the Deputy Commissioner of the Metropolitan Police accepted a directorship with National Car Parks even though the firm was the subject of a criminal investigation. Sir John said, 'Senior police officers routinely have contact with a large number of companies, always with a set of well understood guidelines.'[38]

Some activities are 'illegal' whilst others are controlled by licencing. It therefore pays many businessmen to develop special relationships with senior police officers.

Some of the interrelationships at a social level between legal and illegal business, top police chiefs and wealthy criminals exist in societies such as the masons or the Buffaloes. The porn businessman Humphreys,

> dined with the Buffaloes Association at the Criterion Restaurant. They had sat at the same table as a number of senior detectives.[39]

The masons provide the social milieu where these types of relationships can flourish and mutual favours be exchanged. The author Stephen Knight estimated in 1981 that more than 60 percent of all chief constables were Freemasons.[40]

The bent copper protects crooks and individual members of the ruling class. He incorporates into his work the capitalist ethos and values. He isn't a deviant, but a conformer. His crime is being found out. The Knapp Commission which investigated corruption in the New York police in the early 1970s, explained that not all police take bribes but,

> even those who themselves engage in no corrupt activities are involved in corruption in the sense that they take no steps to prevent what they know or suspect to be going on about them.[41]

The report classified corrupt policemen into 'meat eaters' and 'grass eaters'. The meat eaters aggressively used their powers for material gains. The 'grass eaters' simply accepted pay offs that came their way. The 'meat eaters' got big pay offs from organised syndicates, the 'grass eaters' got smaller sums from small time gambling operations, building contractors wanting to get round regulations and garages making unneeded repairs to cars towed away.

The institutionalised 'clean ups' that sometimes follow exposures are contained from above. New police chiefs may pledge themselves to the necessity of polishing up tarnished images. But when the Hong Kong Independent Commission Against Corruption conducted its inquiry this observation was made:

> Any corrupt system can afford to sacrifice a few heads now and again. It can even use an anti corruption agency as a means of getting rid of people who represent problems whether because they are honest, or because, although corrupt, they are endangering the system through incompetence, greed or attempting to set up on their own.[42]

Inquiries therefore tend to be tightly controlled to see that business can go on as usual, albeit with a cleaner face. Scotland Yard has a long history of such anti corruption drives:

> In 1877 it was revealed that practically every member of the detective department at Scotland Yard up to and including the second in command was in the pay of a vicious gang of swindlers and in 1878 the plain clothes department was completely reorganised with the setting up of the modern CID.[43]

During the 1970s there were four major inquiries and purges in London. Each seemed to follow a similar pattern: a journalistic leak, an investigation, the investigator eased out of the force (often to a company directorship) and one or two officers charged or disciplined.

In the early 1970s the Drug Squad at Scotland Yard was disbanded. The same thing happened to the Obscene Publications Squad. The latter was described in court by Justice Jones in 1977 as a 'vast protection racket' with the biggest and wealthiest operators of porn in Soho deeply involved with Yard officers. The various investigations simply shifted the area of police enterprise. For example, a big upheaval occurred between 1973 and 1976 under Commissioner Robert Mark. A total of 82 officers were sacked and another 301 left during criminal or disciplinary enquiries.[44] After this spring clean Robert Mark shifted the Scotland Yard emphasis away from drugs and porn to the investigation of armed robberies. What happened next was inevitable: the police got heavily involved in armed robbery. A newspaper reported:

> A particularly violent armed robber got married in South London a few years ago. Some of London's heaviest criminals listened to the telegrams read out at the reception. The most popular came from a bent squad of detectives, 'Best wishes from one good firm to another,' it said.[45]

Operation Countryman spent 'nearly four years and 4 million pounds trying to get to the bottom of the scandal behind the telegram'.[46] By 1978 it had compiled allegations against 78 officers from Scotland Yard and 18 from the City of London police. In the end less than half a dozen went to court and by 1982 convictions had been gained against only two officers.[47] By the early 1980s it was reported that 'The firm within a firm carried on business as usual'.[48]

As Operation Countryman was being wound down in the late 1970s and early 1980s other police forces in Britain were also involved in a tangled web of inquiries into each other. In 1982 the Chief Constable of Cheshire was looking into allegations of misconduct in Humberside. Humberside was conducting investigations into allegations about members of the South Yorkshire drug squad and in turn this investigation had gone rancid and was being looked into by the Merseyside Police.

The framing of innocent people, fabrication of evidence and lies on oath led to the wrongful imprisonment of four people for 15 years for the IRA bombing in Guildford. But it wasn't just low ranking constables who framed the Guildford Four. When the convictions were finally declared unsafe, Sir Peter Imbert, the Metropolitan Police Commissioner, spoke to the press about his personal role in the affair. He,

> had no regrets about his personal conduct as the intelligence officer of the Bomb Squad responsible for assessing information about the IRA... In 1974 Sir Peter was part of the Metropolitan Police interviewing team which questioned the Guildford suspects about the Woolwich bombing.[49]

In 1989 the whole of the West Midlands Regional Crime Squad was disbanded amid accusations of forced confessions and tampering with evidence. Some cases were referred to the Police Complaints Authority. Others prompted disciplinary measures. At least one of the disbanded squad was involved in fitting up the Birmingham Six.

The police do not stand outside society correcting the obscene distortions of human behaviour that the capitalist system creates. They are a part of that system. They participate in its markets, share its profits and reinforce its racist behaviour and sexist attitudes.

Are there straight coppers? Nobody can be a member of the force without being aware of the corruption. Those who 'blow the whistle' are forced out. The force is corrupt because it is based on fraud. The fraud is that it is a neutral force preventing crime and serving the interests of all. In reality its role is to protect a corrupt system.

Chapter four

Bread and batons—
police and class struggle

BECAUSE THE English bourgeois finds himself reproduced in his law, as he does in his God, the policeman's truncheon which, in a certain measure, is his own club has for him a wonderfully soothing power. But for the working man quite otherwise.[1]

So Frederick Engels described the police in 1847. Capitalism had created a powerful new working class, who were beginning to exercise their collective strength. The first police were created not to prevent crime but to control this working class and protect the interests of capital.

One of the aims of the Chartists, the great working class movement of the nineteenth century, was to take back some of the fruits of their labour, some of the wealth they had created.

The magistrate Patrick Colquhoun, 'the inventor of the modern police system', spoke for the other side.[2] He helped to organise the Thames Police, wrote an important treatise in 1795 on the 'Police of the Metropolis' and had this to say from the side of capital:

Poverty ... is the most necessary and indispensable ingredient of society... It is the lot of man... it is the source of wealth since without poverty there would be no labour and without labour there would be no riches, no comfort and no benefit to those who may be possessed of wealth.[3]

His concept of a modern police force was related to his understanding that wealth arose from the fact of poverty, the poor had to be controlled and the interests of labour and capital were in conflict.

The British uniformed police is not an ancient institution. It dates from the establishment of the Metropolitan Police in 1829. The word 'police' itself was not used very much in the early eighteenth century in Britain. Writing in 1720 the Scottish hack journalist Edward Burt asked:

> How can you expect order among these people who do not have such a word as Police in their language.[4]

'Police' was then a word used of plain clothes agents in France associated with spying, violence and oppression. There was no modern police force in England, but the wealthy did have a whole apparatus of terror and coercion which was used to halt possible insurrection.

In the late eighteenth and early nineteenth century both before and immediately after Robert Peel's Metropolitan Police Act of 1829 the courts, the gallows, transportation and the army made up the apparatus of terror upon which the ruling class depended to maintain its order. The 'gallows groaned'. Between 1750 and 1769, 909 offenders were capitally convicted—meaning they could be sentenced to death.[5] The number of capital offences grew from about 50 to over 200 between 1688 and 1820.[6] Torture was used and militants could be transported. Even anonymous protest was an offence punishable by death in the acts of 1723 and 1754. Yet that ultimate deterent was not sufficent to curtail all popular protest.

A range of terror laws were passed by the British parliament in the wake of the French Revolution. Most forms of popular political activity were criminalised. The Combination Acts in 1799 made trade unions illegal. Meetings of more than 50 people were against the law and criticism of the government or army could lead to arrest for seditious libel. Freedom of the press was curtailed by heavy taxes on newspapers and imprisonment without trial was legal.

But in spite of the terror laws and special courts, the new industrial working class was beginning to organise effectively and the town 'mob' or demonstration and the strike or 'turn out' were feared by the ruling class. Despite the restrictions, enormous demonstrations were held for economic and political demands. The manufacturers turned first to the army to deal with such resistance. However, the use of the military involved a whole number of problems. There was the question of accommodation. Troops billetted with working class families could prove unreliable. The property owners, alarmed by the symptoms of rebellion in the counties with large manufacturing populations, turned to the government with requests for barracks near to the industrial centres:

> This request was made from 1792 onwards by the wealthy inhabitants of Manchester, Birmingham, Sheffield, Coventry, Northampton and Nottingham ... In 1792 all barracks accommodated 20,000 men. By 1805 there was room for 160,000.[7]

> By the summer of 1812 there were more than 12,000 troops in the disturbed areas, a veritable army, larger than many actual armies with which British Generals have waged and won important foreign campaigns.[8]

The demand for barracks created a boom in the building industry:

> During the Napoleonic wars 155 barracks were built in England for armies to be stationed in the disaffected areas... In 1812 the Parliament gave the go-ahead for the biggest burst of barrack building in British history. Barracks were built at Regents Park, London for 138,000 soldiers, Liverpool 82,000, Bristol 60,000 and Brighton 20,000.[9]

The barracks, however, did not solve the problem of possible disaffection of the soldiers and the fact that they might sympathise with popular discontent. The ordinary soldiers were badly paid, often pressed into service and disciplined by flogging. There was a further tactical problem. In the massive demonstrations of the first half of the nineteenth century, there could be hundreds of thousands on the streets. Soldiers were trained to kill. Killing in such situations could spark off insurrection. The ruling class learned this when they sent in a force of part-time soldiers, the Yeomanry, to break up a peaceful demonstration at St Peter's Field, Manchester in 1819.

The Yeomanry were recruited from the propertied and landowning class and were hated for it. They charged drunkenly into the 80,000 strong demonstration and killed 11 people, one of them a child, and injured hundreds of others. This action did not subdue the workers, it angered them and was followed by a wave of strikes and protests. Unlike most examples of crude ruling class violence, 'Peterloo'—as it became known—is included in school history books, possibly because the wealthy felt there was a lesson to be learned from the working class reaction to the massacre.

From bullets to batons

CLEARLY the old tactics of killing, transporting or executing could prove counter productive against large numbers of organised workers. The days had gone when a judge could calculate how many rioters needed to be executed to put down popular uprisings. The Tory theorist Edmund Burke had made the recommendation that 'six executions with maximum publicity'[10] was about right for quelling agricultural riots. But the urban working class was a different matter.

The political arithmetic of the class struggle was changing. The huge crowds, sometimes up to 50,000 strong, which gathered for public executions came to represent a threat. By 1841 only murder and treason remained capital offences. Edwin Chadwick, regarded as the 'zealous engineer of the industrialist' argued for a different approach. He pointed out the advantages of using a police force instead of soldiers to break up demonstrations.

> Of the military force, it may be observed that the private soldier has both his hands occupied with a musket with which his efficient stabbing action is by the infliction of death by firing or stabbing. The constable or policeman whose weapon is his truncheon or on desperate occasions a cutlass, has one hand at liberty to seize and hold his prisoner, whilst the other represses force by force.[11]

The new policeman would be able to exercise summary punishment with his truncheon without providing martyrs to inflame working class anger. The police could arrest the ring leaders only, a tactic which appeared to be more practical given the numbers of workers they were facing.

Not all the ruling class were enthusiastic about the idea. The question of introducing such a force had been debated and rejected in Parliamentary Committees in 1770, 1793, 1812 and

1818. Who would control it? Who would pay for it? How extensive would its investigative powers be? Even after Peterloo the Parliamentary Committee of 1822 rejected the idea of a police force on the following grounds:

> It is difficult to reconcile an effective system of police with that perfect freedom and exemption from interference, which are the great privilege and blessings of society in this country.[12]

Such ruling class qualms were soon snuffed out, however, when workers tried to exercise their 'freedom' to strike. In time it became clear that an efficient police force could be used to frustrate strikers by protecting scab labour. As manufacturer Thomas Ashton from Hyde said to the Royal Commission:

> In the case of turn outs it would be desirable to have a force to protect the people that are willing to work.[13]

Despite all previous opposition, the ruling class closed ranks when faced with real working class militancy and organisation. The Metropolitan Police Bill of 1829 went through parliament with little opposition. There was one slight stumbling block. The City of London merchants and bankers were worried about police interference with business because the border between theft, deception and legitimate business deals was a line they wished to draw without outside interference. The police in the City were therefore kept as a separate body. They are still separate today.

The Metropolitan Police was based on regimental organisation with divisions and companies. Heading them as Commissioners were a military man, Rowan, and a lawyer, Maine. The debate about whether they should be uniformed or not was resolved by giving them distinctive civilian dress of a top hat strengthened with a thick leather crown and tail coat.[14]

They were to be armed with truncheons and cutlasses when the occasion demanded it. The truncheons could be used for baton charges as advocated by the 'radical reformer' Francis Place, who argued that although outnumbered, the police could break up demonstrations by attacking first,

> on the theory that attack was the best method of defence and that it was better to charge an aggressive mob at sight than to wait and be attacked by it and consequently suffer more

casualties than were inflicted on it.[15]

The new police were not welcomed on the streets. In London on 9 November 1829 posters announced an anti-police demonstration in the following manner:

LIBERTY OR DEATH! BRITONS!! AND HONEST MEN!!!
The time has at last arrived. All London meets on Tuesday. We assure you from ocular demonstration that 6,000 cutlasses have been removed from the Tower for the use of Peel's Bloody Gang. Remember the cursed speech from the Throne!! These damned Police are now to be armed. Englishmen, will you put up with this?[16]

A police constable named Robert Culley was killed in one early baton charge against a demonstration at Cold Bath Field in 1833. Public hostility to the police was such that a jury found a verdict of justifiable homicide.

The Metropolitan Police were used as a mobile riot squad around the country but were successfully fought off in a number of areas. In Birmingham for example opposition to a force of Metropolitan officers reached such a pitch that in July 1839 it broke into open riot and street fighting. Nor did it stop at that. A meeting of citizens immediately after the affair declared that the police were there, not to preserve peace but to infringe the liberties of the people of Birmingham. It called them a 'bullying and unconstitutional force'.[17] The Metropolitan Police were also chased out of Dewsbury: 'the boys of that noble town sent them home again.'[18] Some of the Chartist leaders were very clear in their opposition to the new police. One speaker told a meeting:

If we had a House of Commons composed of working men, they would not have voted £60,000 for the London police and then sent them to annoy and disturb the inhabitants in the remotest districts of the Kingdom.[19]

The challenge of the Chartists

THE CHARTISTS were organising on a national scale. Fear of revolution led the Whig Party to abandon their previous opposition to the extension of the police across the country. The troops and the Metropolitan Police could not alone repress a wide scale insurrection. Police historian Charles Reith explains:

> In 1830 and during most of 1831 the New Police proved that they could control riots in London without military aid... For nearly thirty years the extremist Radicals and other revolutionary leaders had been fully aware of certain facts which exasperated them. The government could suppress riots, but only by moving troops from place to place throughout the country where riots occurred. The total forces at the Government's disposal were hopelessly inadequate if outbreaks occurred or could be made to occur in a number of areas simultaneously.[20]

The 1831 Special Constables Act empowered magistrates to nominate citizens to be enrolled for police duties during emergencies. The 1835 Municipal Corporations Act required the new towns to appoint Watch Committees and set up local police forces. There were also powers to appoint Special and Additional constables.

Powerful Chartist demonstrations took place across the country in 1838. These included an estimated 100,000 in Glasgow, 80,000 in Newcastle on Tyne, 300,000 in Manchester, 250,000 in West Yorkshire and 400,000 at Blackwood in Monmouthshire.[21] The very next year county magistrates as well as the towns were empowered to set up forces. The police had been accepted by the middle and ruling classes and a compromise was reached over who should pay for them, with a degree of local control. Working class resistance to their introduction was still considerable. One Chartist speaker, Bronterre O'Brien, saw that,

> there was no law in England except for the seven hundred thousand living on rents, profits and interest who attempted to govern England by physical force.
> When these minions attack the people they create a riot ... these ruffians should be in gaol instead of peaceable people.[22]

When it was put to another Chartist leader, William Lovett, that some police had been injured by weapons in the Birmingham riot his response was:

> I heard that several of them were wounded, and at the same

time thought that the people were justified in repelling such despotic and bloodthirsty power by any and every means at their disposal, because I believe that the institution of a police force is an infringement on the constitution and liberties possessed by our ancestors.[23]

Thus the police were not seen as friendly Bobbies affectionately named after Robert Peel, but as Bloody Peelers: hired thugs. The new county police were fought off the streets in some places. For example the cotton weavers in Colne in Lancashire drove the police out of town time and again from April to August 1840 until eventually they were installed by the military.[24] In other areas magistrates were reluctant to set up police forces under the 1839 Act because of the expense. They preferred to rely on part time 'specials' or on help from the Metropolitan Police and permanent military establishments. For example, Staffordshire magistrates were compelled by the government to set up a County Constabulary in 1842 to combat the Chartists' general strike. As one historian has argued:

> From the Home Office papers in the Public Record Office it is possible to trace the precise steps by which this renewed Chartist activity directly paved the way to the creation of a major county constabulary.[25]

The mayors and magistrates wanted a 'permanent military' force to be sent to the Potteries; they even offered to pay the cost of providing temporary barracks for them. But the Home Secretary said:

> I will give no pledge, that any given amount of military force will be maintained permanently in any one place. But I can say that I will not allow the troops to remain for any length of time in Billets, and that unless an adequate Police Force be provided in the Potteries, the military must be withdrawn since they cannot be allowed to supply the place of the constables.[26]

A force several hundred strong were established a few months later. In the 1840s, despite the new police forces, the ruling class still depended heavily on the military. The flying pickets of the 1842 general strike (often called the Plug Plot strikes) were met by a motley collection of the new police, police Specials and the military. For example in Leeds:

17 August 1842...First sign of trouble was contained in a report that a large body of men had stopped mills at Farnley and Wortley, had gone to Pudsey for reinforcements, and intended to attack mills at Armley. The forces of law and order set off from the Court House to intercept the mob. First came a large body of police on foot, armed with cutlasses and heavy batons, and led by the Chief Constable, Mr Read, on horseback. They were followed by approximately 1,200 Special constables, walking three and four abreast, and all carrying heavy batons. The armed force brought up the rear—a troop of the 17th Lancers, 18 men of the 87th Infantry with fixed bayonets, a party of the Royal Horse Artillery with a mounted field piece, and finally the Ripon Troop of Yeomanry.[27]

The installation of a force with 'less than lethal violence' was not a sudden process. On occasions sections of the early police wore arms such as cutlasses or pistols. For example, at the Kennington Common demonstration in London on 13 March 1848, 'Five thousand police were in attendance; eighty were mounted and armed with sabres and pistols'[28]. A week earlier five persons were shot in Glasgow on the order of the Superintendant of Police.[29]

Nevertheless, the numbers of Chartist demonstrators killed and imprisoned in relation to the numbers involved was much lower than was the case with earlier agricultural risings.[30] The authorities dared not carry out a sentence of execution on the arrested Chartist leaders Frost, Williams and Jones. In the words of a Chartist poem, 'Fear of Labour's revenge, stayed the hangman's hand'.[31]

The army and police did not necessarily operate in happy unison. On the contrary, there was often open hostility. Fights arose if the police attempted to arrest soldiers. In Leeds a riot which had started in that way lasted for three days and continued long after the soldiers had been called back to barracks. In the anti police riots of the 1840s, 'Off duty soldiers often acted as the spark which ignited a local working class crowd and encouraged them to engage in disturbances'.[32] Such disturbances occurred in Leeds, Hull and Manchester as well as in smaller towns. The instruction was therefore sent out to the police forces that they were not to arrest soldiers who were drunk.

The build up of police over the second half of the nineteenth century gradually created forces which could terrorise, injure, selectively arrest, and break up large assemblies of people without killing and risking escalating the strike action or extending urban rioting. In 1856 the extension of policing across the country was completed by the counties being obliged to set up forces.

Technically, a whole number of different forces were set up under different acts: the Metropolitan Police under the 1829 and 1839 Acts; the City of London Police set up by local Act and Charter; the constabularies in the boroughs under the Municipal Corporations Act 1835; and the forces established in Counties and Boroughs under the 1839 Act and 1856 Acts. The new police had little to do with crime prevention and everything to do with what the ruling class saw as public order. But what was that order about? The Chartist leader Lowery,

> was for peace, law and order; but he would have no peace with oppression and injustice ... Nor would he call that order which gave one man £10,000 as pay for doing nothing, while the working man could only get ten shillings per week. That was disorder and robbery. Their enemies said they had nothing to lose. Why they had produced everything, and if they had got nothing someone must have robbed them most infamously.[33]

Thus the police were seen as protecting ruling class disorder and gross inequality. They were seen as protecting the crimes of the exploiting class. In early police reports there was little pretence that they were concerned with preventing crime as it is defined today. They were about suppressing resistance, controlling the urban poor, arresting for drunkenness, prostitution and vagrancy.

A well ordered life

PROFITS COME from labour. Just as the police attack those who stop the flow of profits by striking, they also make it their business to degrade others not producing profits because they are out of work. Today both unemployed and sick pedestrians are more likely to be stopped by the police than those with jobs.[34]

Historically, homeless vagrants have been subject to particular abuse. They have either to be coerced into labour or criminalised and individually held to blame for their poverty. For example in the nineteenth century vagrants were seen as 'a challenge and an offence to the ethos of the period'.[35] The Vagrancy Act of 1824 was really directed against,

> a disorderly way of living... people ought to be prevented by law from following an idle disorderly mode of life... it is the *mode of life* that is aimed at, not a particular act.[36]

The modern police arose alongside the 'criminalisation' of poverty enshrined in the 1834 Poor Law. This was basically calculated to coerce people into wage labour by refusing outdoor relief to the able bodied and forcing them into the work house if they failed to sell their labour. One of the early architects of the police system, Edwin Chadwick, the darling bureaucratic representative of the industrialists, was also the instigator and designer of the 1834 Poor Law. Chadwick noted that the new Poor Law needed the aid of a strong police force:

> He pointed out how badly a rural police was needed, not only to deal with beggars, vagrants and casuals, but 'for the suppression of tumults connected with the adminstration of relief'.[37]

The Chartists protested that, 'The police would be "blue butchers" sent into the country to enforce the poor laws'.[38] And so they were. The county police were given the task of controlling the footloose soldiers returning from the Crimea and 'ticket of leave' men who had been convicted but could no longer be transported. The suppression of vagrancy was the preamble and the justification of the County and Borough Police Act of 1856.[39] Significantly, one of the new Government Inspectors of Constabulary, Major William Cartwright, had been Chairman of a Poor Law Union. He insisted the function of the police was to separate the 'criminal tramper' from the respectable working man, tramping in search of work. 37 out of 43 English counties employed their police as poor law relieving officers for ten years or more between 1856 and 1880. The procedure for controlling the mobile poor was as follows:

As vagrants entered a town or village they were directed by the policeman on the beat to the police station... the respectable were sent on to the overseer and the 'criminal' were retained.[40]

The 1824 Vagrancy Act, which survived into the 1990s, contained the charge:

That you did wander abroad and lodge in a certain barn (*or* in an outhouse, *or* in the open air *or* under a tent *or* in a wagon) ... and not give a good account of yourself...[41]

Hounding travellers and vagrants supported the wage labour ethos. The police attempted to clear the streets of trading activities and entertainers who were the survivors of a pre-industrial economy. Play was often associated with market days. Feast days and holidays were also trading days. In one early example it was reported that, 'the fairs at Stepney, Hampstead, West End, and Peckham had been crushed by the police, that "stern rugged nurse of national morality".'[42] The historian EP Thompson said that in the nineteenth century,

In general the police were impartial, attempting to sweep off the streets with an equal hand street traders, beggars, prostitutes, street entertainers, pickets, children playing football and free thinking and socialist speakers alike. The pretext, very often, was that a complaint had been received from a shopkeeper. William Morris remarked on the impatience of 'the more luxurious part of society' to 'clear the streets of costermongers, organs, processions and lecturers of all kinds, and make them a sort of decent prison corridor, with people just trudging to and from work'.[43]

'Force, fraud and good will'

THE CONTROL of the massive labour force at home was crucial to British capitalists in the third quarter of the nineteenth century when the world map showed the spreading bloody red of the British Empire. They were brutal in their imperial expansion but much more nervous about the use of violence at home as they were aware of the revolutionary potential of the working class. Gladstone told an aristocratic relative:

Please to recollect, we have to govern millions of hard hands; that it must be done by force, fraud or good will.[44]

The father of the modern police, Robert Peel, had explained why the 'good will' was necessary:

I do feel that the point at which we all ought to strive is to improve the conditions and elevate the feelings of the great labouring classes. I tell you it is not safe unless you do it.[45]

The period between 1850 and 1880 was relatively calm, but there were still major demonstrations. Large street meetings were seen as a threat and for a time the ruling class tried to ban them. However, such crude tactics proved difficult to implement, as was shown by the struggle over the Sunday Trading Bill.

Demonstrations were called in Hyde Park in June and July 1855 in protest against government attempts to restrict trading and other activities on Sundays. Workers were paid late on Saturdays and needed Sunday trading. Hyde Park was chosen as the venue because it was the Sunday playground of the rich. The police had been unable to prevent an earlier demonstration and on 1 July 1855 a major police intervention went wrong:

To make up for their humiliation the previous week they conducted what appeared to be a very well planned terror exercise to break up the end of the demonstration ... the police were in need of bloody heads and arrests in order not to fall from the sublime to the ridiculous without some intermediate link.[46]

Troops were brought in to back up the police, but the soldiers, just back from the disease ridden bloodiness of the Crimea, proved unreliable. The military were cheered and welcomed by the crowd as heroes, and instead of backing the police the soldiers turned on them for brutalising the workers. The people shouted,

'Long live the army', 'Down with the police', 'down with the Sunday Bill' ... a sergeant of the Guards came up and ... calmed down the soldiers and persuaded some of them to follow him to the barracks. But most of the soldiers remained right there in the midst of the crowd gave vent to their fury against the police in unrestrained measure.[47]

Faced with a split in its forces and mass demonstrations that looked insurrectionary, the government accepted defeat and withdrew the Sunday Trading Bill. Concession was a tactic that the Victorian ruling class were to learn during the years of economic expansion.

Police history between 1850 and 1880 is best understood in the context of the discovery of the conservative possibility of parliamentary democracy.

Consider the problems encountered in handling the campaign for the reform of parliament. The Reform League was initially set up under the influence of Karl Marx and workers' groups involved in the 'First International'. The International Working Men's Association, based in London, was seen as a gesture of international solidarity by British union leaders, but under the influence of Karl Marx its object became the greater one of uniting workers of all countries in the class struggle. The Reform League had no such revolutionary aims.

The Reform League soon came to emphasise only two of the old Chartist demands: for male suffrage (although they qualified it) and ballot voting. The movement for parliamentary reform was soon to be financed by manufacturers and it lost most of its radicalism. However, there was still mass involvement. Demonstrations 150,000 to 200,000 strong took place in London. Some on the hard right of the ruling class wanted to move in with police and troops on every occasion but the 'statesmen' of the period were much more cautious.

In July 1866 a reform meeting in Hyde Park was banned. Sixteen hundred constables, mounted and on foot, were stationed at the gates to stop a march entering the park.[48] The leaders tried to divert it away to Trafalgar Square but the demonstration, 'huge, swaying and shouting', did not move off. As the numbers grew,

> every instant seemed to threaten wholesale suffocation unless the pressure were relaxed. Suddenly the iron railings bent and cracked, either from the exertion of intentional force... or else from the ... movement of the crowd. The barriers down, a vast body of men poured through the breaches, many injuries were received, and the police ... came tumbling up from the main gates and charged the struggling mass with drawn truncheons. They might as well have charged the Falls of Niagara.[49]

Finding themselves overpowered, the police sent for assistance... the soldiers received quite an ovation from the people in the Park. Cries of 'Three cheers for the Guards— the people's Guards!' were raised and warmly taken up... Amid loud and prolonged cheers the soldiers marched and wheeled and marched again; but the crowd seemed quite confident that there would be no firing and no resort to cold steel. The commanding officer possessed more discretion than the Home Secretary, otherwise Peterloo might have been re-enacted on a hundredfold larger scale. But after watching the soldiers for a short time the crowd gradually and without uproar dispersed, and the park was left in quiet.[50]

Skirmishes between police and workers in the park went on for days afterwards and the Home Secretary was eventually forced to persuade the reform leaders to clear the park as police and soldiers couldn't do so. But when a new Tory government came in the middle class Reform League leadership became more willing to challenge them. Another Hyde Park meeting was planned on 6 May. The cabinet published a notice that,

the use of the Park for the holding of such meeting is not permitted... now all persons are hereby warned and admonished to abstain from attending, aiding or taking part in such meeting. Signed by the Home Secretary Walpole.[51]

The proposal to defy the government was won at a Reform League meeting, but the leaders tried to undermine the demonstration, insisting that it was not to be a confrontation, just a show of 'moral strength':

Come without bands or banners ... meet ... in your moral strength until you are ungrudgingly invested with ... the right to vote in the choice of those who make your laws, impose your taxes, govern your country and exercise rule over your properties, your liberties and your lives... The question is not one of party and ought not to be one of class.[52]

Contrast with this the detailed preparation of the state forces on the other side:

Altogether more than 10,000 men, police and military, were kept ready to move and close in upon the park within half an hour's notice.[53]

In the event, the demonstration was 100,000 to 150,000 strong. The government dared not use its forces. The ban on the Hyde Park meeting was withdrawn. The police and troop build up had been an ineffective exercise in sabre rattling.

It was not the fear of being unable to disperse the crowd that made the astute government back down, it was the possibility of changing a reformist movement into an insurrectionary one. Deals with middle and working class leaders were more efficient and less dangerous than physical confrontation. The Government back down was seen as a real victory and established the right of meeting and public speaking in Hyde Park for generations to come. Having lost face, the Home Secretary was forced to resign and the bill prohibiting meetings in the park was dropped:

> A humiliation had been suffered; a humiliation which gave notice that henceforth 'goodwill' rather than 'force' or 'fraud' was to be the main instrument... After 6 May Hyde Park gradually became an established tradition. It stood for freedom in relation to the pretensions of aristocratic privilege, but it also stood for the powerlessness of enthusiasts.[54]

The extension of the parliamentary vote was also granted to a large section of the working class in 1867 at a time when they had little revolutionary aspiration. Some bourgeois politicians were well aware that the divisions within the working class could be welded together with speed if force and excessive terror were seen to be used against the class as a whole. Karl Marx also understood how police or more particularly military violence could 'knock some class solidarity into the skulls of the degenerate labour aristocrats and conservative English workers'.

Labour leaders

THE ECONOMIC boom from the 1850s onwards made possible the granting of wage increases and improved conditions to sections of workers, so that industrial demands could be isolated from political demands.[55] The nature of trade unionism also changed in this period. From 1850 onwards powerful craft unions emerged along with union leaders prepared to do deals and control their members. Full time paid officials came to see their interests as sometimes different from those of their members. These new bureaucrats depended on the union for strength, yet hated any threat to industrial stability.

There was concern that 'good relationships' with the craftsmen should not be upset by untactful policing. Home Secretary Matthews made this comment in respect of a Reform march consisting mainly of skilled craftsmen:

> These men are the pick of the working classes, perfectly orderly... It would be disastrous to get the police into collisions with them.[56]

From 1850 onwards the new craft union leaders presented no challenge to the system. They embraced the competitive ideas of capitalism, were highly selective about their membership and reduced the necessity for policing by discouraging strikes, solidarity and any form of violent confrontation. The 'model' engineering union, the Amalgamated Society of Engineers, whose membership rose from 5,000 in 1851 to 44,032 in 1875[57] was much praised by the ruling class. ASE leader Allan was to declare: 'We believe that all strikes are a complete waste of money not only in relation to the workmen, but also to the employers'.[58]

These 'model' unions charged high dues and centralised control of their membership. Little of their money was used to support strikes. The leaders did not like to see their funds reduced by strike action. The model unions could exert a similar sort of control by withholding benefits as the state was subsequently to operate.[59]

In the 1860s the ruling class agonised over whether unions were a good thing or not. Clearly in so far as they were curbing labour militancy they were of use. This was spelt out by members of the commission set up to investigate the unions:

> It seems, however, that whilst the union gives an increased power of striking, it brings an *increased sense of orderly subordination and reflection*... and furthermore the effect of the established societies is to diminish the frequency and certainly the disorder of strikes.[60]

If union leaders were forced by rank and file pressure to use their huge funds to support national strikes, the police would then be necessary to prevent effective picketing:

Whilst recommending that the law relating to voluntary combinations for the disposal of labour and capital should be relaxed to the extent that we have proposed we deem it of the highest moment that the law, so far as it aims at repressing all coercion of the will of others in the disposal of their labour or capital, should be in no degree relaxed.[61]

The craft unions, with their vast funds, were to be given legal status. However, practically everything which would make strike action effective was to be criminal.

So legal protection was afforded to union funds in the 1871 Trade Union Act. But at the same time it became easier for police to arrest pickets for the slenderest of reasons under the Criminal Law Amendment Act of the same year. Where unions did get involved in a fight, the police would be able to call on extensive powers. The Act extended these so much that in 1871, 'Seven women were imprisoned in South Wales merely for saying "bah" to one blackleg'.[62] Workers' mobilisations forced the government to repeal the Act, making picketing legal in 1875. But by that time the Great Depression was considerably undermining the bargaining power of the craft unions.

This theme of the use of the trade union bureaucracy keeps recurring in the subsequent history of the British police in the

Figure 3. Police numbers 1856-90.[63]

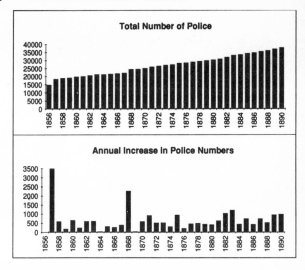

class struggle. It is a theme recognised in the 1867 commission by the coal magnate Lord Elcho who in his questioning of Alexander MacDonald, president of the Miners' National Association, found the trade unionist talked about two sorts of authority. One is exercised by the police and army under the authority of the magistrates. But there is also 'another authority, such as the authority of the heads of unions'[64] who could use 'their influence to calm the men and get them back to work again'.[65]

The Victorian policeman in the boom years was a comic music hall figure because in the 25 years after 1850 they were not the most essential part of the ruling class's mechanism of control. It may be argued that between 1850 and 1875 the policeman performed an important ideological role in stigmatising and dividing workers but proved less useful than had been originally envisaged in dealing with mass protest. Through most of this period police numbers grew only steadily. The exceptional years were 1857, when the state feared the return of soldiers from the Crimea War, and 1867, following the Reform Act disturbances at Hyde Park.

Other, more sophisticated methods of control were used as the idea of reforming capitalism replaced ideas of revolution and the class struggle ebbed. The situation was reversed again, however, with the great struggles of the 1880s.

Limits to the law

IN GREAT BRITAIN, especially as the foremost producing nation of the world, labour quarrels have been more frequent, on a larger scale and more perniciously fought out, than elsewhere. Here the fighting organisations of masters and men have been the most highly developed...[66]

Working class solidarity and organisation reached magnificent heights in the dock strike of 1889. It involved grass roots organisation among the unskilled on a scale that the state could not handle. It followed hard upon a bloody clearance of unemployed workers from Trafalgar Square and the 1888 Matchgirls' strike in East London.

The strike for the dockers' tanner, as it was called, created insoluble problems for the police. There was heavy internal policing within the docks, each of which had its own force. For example, in the West and East India docks, of the total of 1,070 regularly employed, 100 were police.[67] It is a measure of the cohesion of workers involved in the strike that these dock police were almost irrelevant.

Mass picketing was crucial to the strike's success. The number of pickets was at one stage reckoned to be in the region of 15,000 and there were daily marches from the docks to the City, one of the biggest reaching 100,000. According to the **Times** 'the struggle was kept up day and night by relays of men watching the gates'.[68]

There were certainly police around. Burns, one of the strike leaders, spoke of 2,000 police being on duty but commented that they hadn't been used.[69] The dockers sent back scab labour brought up from Southampton and a few days later it was stated that 60 men taken to the Royal Albert docks from Scotland had 'joined the men on strike and forty three of them were in the procession today.'[70] A letter was sent to the **Times** fretting about the fact that the police were able to do nothing and hinting at an appeal for army intervention.[71]

The strike was spreading like a fire to other workers so that by 29 August, 'The strikers with their families amount to at least one tenth of the entire population of the capital.'[72] Burns was able to sneer at suggestions that the leaders should be arrested: 'if this was not so serious a proposal it would be contemptible, ridiculous and comical.'[73] So superior was the strikers' organisation that they had a steam tug to contest control of the river with the police's rowing boats.[74]

It was only when the strike was nearing its successful if untidy end that there were any newspaper reports of police violence. The Metropolitan Commissioner's annual report for 1889 contained only one minute reference to the dock strike, about police awards: 'Two commendations for zeal, firmness and discretion displayed during the strike of dock labourers.'[75]

It wasn't that the police were too few to be of any use. At the time there were 14,490 Metropolitan officers and 774 dockyard police.[76] They might have been hard pressed to take on the pickets when they were tens of thousands strong, but tactically it was discretion that was the order of the day. The strike escalated too rapidly for the authorities to adopt an aggressive stance. The fear of a general strike across the country was too great. The dockers' tanner was won.

The same caution was shown in a strike in 1890 in Leeds. Gas workers successfully prevented scab labour being used to replace them and forced the scabs to leave the town. Elaborate precautions were taken to guard the procession of 250 blacklegs as they approached the area of the gasworks:

> In addition to the police there were foot soldiers and mounted carabineers from the Leeds barracks... masses of people ... lined the streets, surmounted the walls, filled windows and stood on roofs... there extended ... one great turbulent excited mass of humanity, boiling and seething with expectation... not less than 15,000 to 20,000 people... the bridges were crowded with men... piles of missiles... were hurled ... the police, soldiers and cavalry began to charge and while the police used their batons some of the soldiers were shouting to their officers 'let's shoot, let's shoot'.[77]

The soldiers weren't allowed to shoot, even though the effect would have undoubtedly been to disperse the crowd. They were on a 'policing', not a military, exercise. The officers feared escalating the dispute and soldiers and police were rendered impotent by the superior numbers of the strikers and their supporters. The gasworkers won a complete victory.

The killing of workers in struggle hadn't stopped altogether. Lethal weapons were again to be used against strikers during the miners' strike and lock out of 1893. The army opened fire at Featherstone. A socialist pamphlet dubbed the Featherstone killings the 'Peterloo of the wage slaves'. Here's what happened:

> The armed troops moved steadily to Ackton Hall colliery where they were later to bayonet charge the indignant and protesting miners and eventually in the face of stone throwing, to open fire into the thickest portion of the crowd. Two men were killed and sixteen injured as the 'Feather-stone Massacre' was blasted into the already bloody pages of the history of miners and mining.[78]

During this period soldiers were continually used as police back up, but methods were changing to the use of bludgeoning

Figure 4. Police numbers, crimes and strikes.[79]

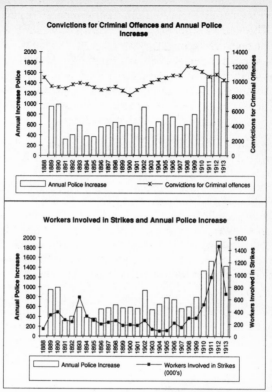

rather than open fire. The police were gradually assuming more importance. Between 1886 and 1890 police numbers rose by 9 percent and continued to rise through the 1890s. In the upsurge of class struggle between 1900 and the outbreak of the First World War police numbers increased by 20 percent.

Figure 4 shows that the annual increase in police numbers has a closer relationship with the level of class struggle than with the level of recorded crime. As the Inspector of Constabularies pointed out:

> The general unrest at home in the years 1909-1913 had emphasised the necessity for expanding the force to meet emergencies too great for its normal strength.[80]

The Great Unrest

WHEN THE Great Unrest, the strike wave of 1909 to 1914 erupted, the ruling class used every force at its disposal to hang on to control, including both the police and the army.

The Welsh coal strike of 1910 involved some 30,000 miners and illustrated the developing function of the police as the main coercive force. The strike was significant because the tactics were determined and centrally directed by the Home Office and taken out of the hands of the mineowners.

The policy was what would now be termed 'Military Action in support of the Civil Power'. Winston Churchill was at the Home Office and Major General Macready from the War Office was put in charge of the combined operation.[81] Police and troops were brought in from several different areas, but the most important contingent came from London.[82] The state forces included 50 mounted police and 2 regiments and 5 companies of soldiers including five troops of cavalry. The Home Office stressed, 'The military are present only to support the police in case of extreme necessity.'[83] Macready seems to have believed he was acting as an impartial umpire, saying 'the work of the police is to maintain order and protect life and property with entire impartiality as between employers and work people'.[84]

Certain employers, however, believed that as they had requisitioned the extra police, they therefore employed them. 'The mine managing class is looked upon by the police as having a kind of authority over them.'[85] In fact there was a division of labour, with Macready responsible for the timing of the introduction of scabs. The Home Secretary said:

> You should remember that the owners are within their legal rights in claiming to import labour, but that you Macready are entitled to judge the time, the manner and circumstances of such importation... to ensure that the authorities responsible for keeping order have adequate forces upon the spot.[86]

There was cautiousness and even Churchill, who called for 'vigorous policing', urged Macready to go easy on the use of troops. The Featherstone shooting was still remembered by Macready as 'unfortunate':

The Ministers Churchill and Haldane, while promising to supply all reasonable assistance in the way of police and military, were insistent that firearms would not be made use of except as a very last resort.[87]

Troops were also used extensively during the railway strike of 1911. But this struggle had significant peculiarities. Railways were particularly vulnerable to sabotage by small groups of strikers and the question of railway unionisation was very sensitive. The railways were seen as strategic as they made possible rapid troop and police movements from one area to another.[88] The historians Beatrice and Sidney Webb noted:

> For a whole generation after the establishment of railways no one appears to have thought Trade Unionism any more permissible among their employees than among the soldiers or the police.[89]

Military style discipline was enforced by an elaborate system of fines and punishments.[90] But unionisation amongst the massive workforce—300,000 in the 1880s—could not be stopped. Successful mass picketing during a railway dispute had provoked the notorious 1902 Taff Vale judgement which allowed employers to sue for losses incurred in a strike.

Churchill feared the rail strike would turn into a general uprising and Whitehall was in a 'state of constant excitement'. Instructions were given that 'all preparations be made for the immediate dispatch of troops to any point where trouble might break out'.[91] A photograph has survived of two policemen and three soldiers with bearskins on their heads guarding not Buckingham Palace but Clapham Junction signal box.[92] 'Practically the whole of the troops in Great Britain were on duty scattered along the railway system'.[93]

The mining and rail strikes were the major elements in a more general upsurge of industrial struggle which was only cooled by the outbreak of the First World War. Still, the First World War put the working class into a very strong position. Prime Minister Lloyd George considered that, 'industrial unrest spelt a graver menace to our endurance and ultimate victory than even the military strength of Germany'.[94]

But capitalists must have been reassured by the way in which the trade union leaders identified with the state's difficulties. They agreed in 1915 to suspend,

> all rules and customs impeding maximum output. Job demarcation, strikes, refusal of overtime, restrictions on night and Sunday working and a good deal of health and safety legislation all went the same way...
> Positions in the government and on official bodies now began to absorb great numbers of officials, making the trade unions and Labour Party virtually organs of state.[95]

There were militant strikes during the war in South Wales and revolutionaries went to gaol for leading struggles in Glasgow. Towards the end of the war the Russian Revolution revived working class confidence and after the guns fell silent, the class war resumed with unequalled ferocity. Again, the dilemma about using troops raised its head. But they dared not use troops against railway workers in the upsurge of 1918:

> The Government which sent soldiers to guard some of its railway stations, hastened to announce publicly, in significant contrast with its decision of 1912—that in no case would the troops be employed to run trains... It was reported that in some cases the soldiers fraternised with the pickets and were promptly withdrawn to barracks; and the Cabinet was certainly warned, by high military authority, against attempting to use troops.[96]

Instead, a different method was used to contain militancy:

> The leaders of the principal Trade Unions indirectly affected by the railway stoppage, notably the various sections of Transport workers, together with officials or representatives of the Miners, the Parliamentary committee, and the Labour Party, had been meeting in anxious conclave, summoned it should be stated by the Executive of the National Transport Workers Federation—with a view to restraining their own members from impetuous action in support of the railwaymen and to bringing pressure to bear on both parties to secure a settlement.[97]

The cowardice of union leaders was central to containing the militancy which reached a high point in 1919. They were again to play a key role in preserving capitalism seven years later during the General Strike.

The General Strike

THE GENERAL Strike, precipitated by a wholesale attack on over a million miners was seen by the ruling class as the key test of its strength over the working class. Millions of workers came out over the nine days in May 1926.

The occasional football match between police and strikers received much publicity, but the veil of history has been drawn over the violent confrontations which did occur. It was because of police batons, not because of friendly sport, that 23 people were taken to hospital in Hull.[98] Violent clashes between police and strikers were reported in Southsea, Swansea, Nottingham, Preston, Edinburgh, Glasgow, Leeds, Newcastle, Chester-le-Street and several places in London. There were confrontations involving head injuries at the entrance of the Blackwall tunnel.[99]

However, given the scale of the 1926 clash, physical confrontations were relatively few. The union leaders bent over backwards to urge cooperation with the police. In Lincoln the police even asked the trades council to 'supply the whole of the special constables'.[100] The trades council agreed![101]

While the TUC prepared nothing in the run up to the strike, the government had laid centralised contingency plans, including the recruitment of Specials whose numbers rose from 7,803 in 1925 to 143,637 in 1926. The number of reserves went up from 3,084 to 87,027. However, it was not these forces which defeated the strike, rather it was the union leaders, who called it off even as it was gaining momentum.[102]

It's worth looking at the Specials as they have historically represented the crudest distillation of class hatred deployed by the British state. In 1926 many Specials were students (at that time part of the social elite), professionals or retired army officers who,

> happily donned the blue and white armband over cricket sweaters or Fair Isle jumpers and drew their truncheons and steel helmets from government stores. The class divisions were clearly drawn and while for the most part it was a question of answering a patriotic call, for many it was a chance to 'teach the blighters a lesson'. Swaggering polo playing ex officers wielded yard long clubs and flourished whips as they cantered in military formation in Hyde Park,

replete with jodphurs and Empire builders helmets.[103]

Clement Attlee (later to become Labour Prime Minster) said of the Special constables in 1923:

> If you start this sort of organisation... which is so like the White Guards, the Ku Klux Klan, the Fascists, which all developed along these lines then you are heading for a revolution, in which you may get violence and in which you will ruin the country altogether.[104]

Attlee overstated the Specials' autonomy from the establishment as they have a long history of representing not only ruling class reserves, but on some occasions their main force. Their role in Northern Ireland has been horrific. In Britain Specials have sometimes been recruited with vulgar haste and armed with weapons ranging from cutlasses to chair legs. They predate the regular police in the provincial county forces. The Special Constables Act was passed in 1831 which empowered justices to conscript men for use against Reform demonstrations.

When it came to the Chartist demonstration in London on 10 April 1848, Specials were enrolled by the thousands. A demonstration of perhaps 200,000 was expected and the Metropolitan Police were only 4,873 strong.[105] The following description gives an idea of who was recruited. The Specials,

> ranged from a bevy of London coal-whippers to the exiled Louis Napoleon ... They included Richard the son of Count Metternich (the economist)... Nassau Senior's daughter recalled 'Every man I knew was a special constable'...'Many of the special constables.. had been more or less pressurised into signing on. Others had signed on in romantic enthusiasm to defend their country and its government from revolution'.[106]

The usefulness of Specials was reiterated by the Home Office in the turbulent year of 1911. A Home Office circular stressed the desirability of having two sets of police reserves, 'the first consisting of men prepared to assume whole time duty for payment, and the second of men prepared to combine part time duty as Special Constables with their ordinary vocations'.[107]

But there was not an inexhaustible supply of Specials. In 1919 the cabinet disagreed as to the ease of recruitment. Some presented upper class optimism on the question. Aukland Geddes pointed to universities 'full of trained men who could co-operate with clerks and stockbrokers' and apparently Bonar Law, an ex Tory Prime Minister, often referred to the stockbrokers as a loyal fighting class to the degree that a cabinet member remarked that, 'one felt that potential battalions of stockbrokers as a loyal fighting force were to be found in every town.'[108]

Others disagreed. Having to build up numbers meant reaching into the working class for recruits:

> Sir Frederick Wodehouse, Assistant Commissioner of Police in 1919 said of the Specials 'those who belonged to the working classes were all Union men and were not to be relied upon'.[109]

Certainly the recruitment of and reliance on Specials was an important aspect of inter war policing. The number of Specials was at its highest in 1926 but even by 1932 there were still 136,340 Specials compared to only 57,319 regular police.[110]

The national force

THE HISTORY of the development of the police in Britain explodes many myths surrounding the force and its function. Britain has long had an armed, dangerous and—when it has suited—lethal police force set up not to protect ordinary people, but to keep them in their place.

One further myth is destroyed by this history of police and class conflict: that Britain has no national police force. Although technically there were a whole number of locally based forces, a high degree of central control was exerted from early on. Only if forces could show the national authorities that they were 'efficient', could they obtain central government funding, initially of 25 percent and subsequently of 50 percent. This central control made possible the honing of police intervention to the most suitable level of violence. The 'centralisation of order maintenance'[111] effectively curbed the eagerness of individual employers to send private police thugs into industrial disputes with 'guns blazing'.

There had been private police forces, 'employed at the charge of private persons'[112] which the employers were keen to let rip, the most important of which were in the docks. But these additional constables were under the orders and discipline of the Chief Constables. For example, in the 1842 general strike the Vice Lieutenant of Staffordshire, the Earl of Dartmouth, asked for 'the two pounder guns and for the muskets kept in Staffordshire County gaol' and sought 'cannon shot and ball cartridges' from government stores.[113] A similar desire to shoot miners down was expressed by some Welsh mineowners in 1898.[114]

As the practice of policing developed, the police acted in the interests of the employing class as a whole and could curb the individual excesses of employers whose actions might easily have led to increased working class anger and the spread of militancy.

In the US, by contrast, there were much more independent and numerous private forces. The US railway policeman or 'Cinder Dick' as he was known, often had a criminal past and the railway companies believed that, 'In times of industrial disturbance ... the black jack and the gun were more effective than the law.'[115] There were also the Coal and Iron police which were, 'in effect little more than cavalry composed of criminals, gun men and bar room drop outs.' Union smashing was a violent service provided by 230 security agencies such as Pinkertons.[116]

In Britain—in the struggles between capital and labour from the dock strike and new unionism of 1889 to the General Strike of 1926—the acceleration in the build up of police and Special numbers can be directly related to upturns in the class struggle and the more sophisticated terror tactic of breaking pickets. However police, Specials and army could still be made powerless by mass organisation of workers with a fighting leadership, as the 1889 dock strike proved. The 1926 General Strike showed that class defeats could happen with little use of the fighting forces of the masters if union leaders were prepared to betray their members.

Chapter five

Class traitors

THE POLICE have assiduously defended the interests of the ruling class ever since their inception. Time and again they have lined up with the bosses. Pickets have been repeatedly attacked.

However, there is an obvious peculiarity in this record. Most police officers have little in common with those they defend. The lifestyles and incomes of the ruling class—the top half to one percent of the population—bear no relation to those of all but the top police officers. The average police officer, by contrast, is certainly well paid by the standards of most workers, but not enormously so.

This contradiction can present difficulties in understanding the position of the police in capitalism. The commonest approach is to look at the background and lifestyle of the police—drawn mostly from the working class and having a comparable standard of living—and to deduce that they are simply 'workers in uniform'. For example, a century into the brutal history of the Metropolitan Police, left wing Labour leader George Lansbury gave this advice to workers during the 1926 General Strike:

> Don't quarrel with the police. We can and will win without disorder of any kind. Policemen are flesh of our flesh and bone of our bone.[1]

This sentiment has been repeated subsequently by many Labour Party members and denies the obvious role that the police have performed in class struggles, including the General Strike itself. Nor do the police defend the ruling class for the simple reason that at times of heightened class struggle they are paid well above the average wage. There are plenty of other groups of workers on similar pay, including some senior teachers, some white collar workers and even some skilled manual workers. But they do not necessarily identify with the bosses' interests.

Being working class isn't just about pay and lifestyle, but about the necessity of taking collective action to defend wages and conditions. It is about being tied to the necessity to sell labour power and to take orders from other people. In this sense something like 75 percent of the population—including most white collar employees—can be included in the working class. There are also some we might call New Middle Class in management or some professionals who sell their labour but who have a great deal of control over their own lives and exercise considerable power over others. They are in a contradictory class position and in struggle they may be drawn to one side or the other.

Ordinary police and prison officers are unusual employees who don't fit into any of these classes. They may be drawn mainly from the working class but their employment conditions make them unlike other workers. Although they sell their labour and are bullied in a highly authoritarian regime, they exercise enormous powers over others. They are indoctrinated for their day to day activities to stereotype sections of the working class as 'scum' and to treat with the same contempt demonstrators and strikers. Both police and prison officers are usually socially isolated, even off duty.

Their experience of collective action is often in class confrontation as the violent forces of the bosses. This does not draw them nearer to workers but alienates them from the class of their origin. They do not constitute a part of the working class. They are traitors to their class and their loyalty to their new masters is only likely to falter when the power of the bosses is really challenged by a tremendously high level of class struggle.

We shall examine how their historical development has shaped their attitudes and position. But first let us consider one particular occasion at the height of the class struggle when the police did threaten to behave like workers.

Strike

THE YEARS 1918 and 1919 saw strikes and revolutions across Europe. Shock waves from the Russian Revolution, mutinies in the German, French and British armies, together with massive strikes had the ruling classes across Europe trembling in fear. Britain was no exception.

In 1918 there was a growing number of strikes, including those among London bus conductresses, Lancashire millworkers, Welsh railworkers and Yorkshire miners; and the police were drawn into this rising struggle.[2] The National Union of Police and Prison Officers (NUPPO) was formed.

A Metropolitan Police strike involved practically the whole of the force by 30 August 1918. Mass demonstrations were called and the government feared a bad example would be set to the army, particularly if negotiating rights for a police union were recognised. At the time, General Smuts and the Under Secretary of State agreed,

> the men must be got back to work quickly, but they must at the same time avoid recognising the Union. They all thought this could be done by a generous increase in pay and the introduction of some method of dealing with grievances.[3]

A pay increase of 13 percent was given, more than had been demanded. Troops sent to control police demonstrators fraternised with them instead. On addressing a Downing Street demonstration, Lloyd George stated that there could be no recognition of the police union. Years later he told the House of Commons how he considered that at the time, 'This country was nearer to Bolshevism on that day than at any time since'.[4]

The next year the police were used to baton charge a massive demonstration of the National Federation of Discharged Soldiers and Sailors. Union leaders protested to JH Hayes, the General Secretary of the police and prison officers' union and pointed out that by their actions the police had shown that 'They were no friends of the working class.'[5] Hayes's response was:

> the only solution for occurrences of this kind is the democratisation of the police force, the ending of militarism in the Metropolitan force, the full and complete recognition of the Union and the closer linking up of the police with organised labour. As a union we looked upon our comrades in the workshops and from the Army as comrades.[6]

This attitude was probably far to the left of most of the police involved. General Sir Neville Macready who had been brought in as Commissioner to break the police union welcomed the statement because he thought it would turn constables against industrial action. It did however point to a possible identification between police and workers which the authorities feared. The Government were dependent on the police, as Macready said, 'in the event of labour trouble'.[7] It was made clear that an officer could be a policeman or a trade unionist, *not* both. The union threatened a strike in response.

The Commissioner issued an order in May 1919 threatening dismissal with loss of pension rights for any officer failing to report for duty.[8] In the event—because of promises of more pay, threats of suspension and the delaying tactics of Macready—only 2,400 police stopped work. Picketing of other stations was not as successful as it had been the previous year. The numbers were down and Macready had brought in military units. In Liverpool the strike was much stronger. The night in 1919 is remembered as the Great Loot:

> It was a chance to hit back for all the empty bellies, the bare feet, the squalor and four years of war... Even tiny young-sters struggled home with sacks full of groceries.[9]

So nervous were the authorities that 2,000 Specials were enrolled from banks and corporations and a battleship and two destroyers were sent up the River Mersey. Troops with bayonets were sent into Liverpool and one man was shot dead by the soldiers. As there were strikes in the docks and on the trams, the troops remained garrisoned in Liverpool for a further month.[10]

The police strike was crushed. It was weak nationally and there was little support from other unions. The 2,400 strikers were dismissed outright. Amongst the dismissals were 51 percent of the Liverpool and 63 percent of the Birkenhead forces.[11] The Police Act was passed quickly, under which two year jail sentences could be imposed on anyone causing disaffection in the police. The police union was made illegal and replaced by the Police Federation which was designed in such a way that it could never be a proper union.

Representative boards which had been set up after the 1918 strike 'in which constables predominated' were replaced by boards in which equal representation was given to constables, sergeants and inspectors.[12] The new Federation had no proper negotiating rights, and was prevented from having any links with outside bodies. It could not affiliate to the TUC and was thus isolated from the organised labour movement. Initially the Federation was prevented from raising subscriptions from its members which, 'might form the nucleus of a strike fund ... it was obliged to function on a few hundred pounds held on its behalf by the Home Office.'[13]

All Federation officers had to be policemen and thus subject to discipline. It was nicknamed the 'goose club' because its members were guaranteed to march closely in step with the authorities.[14] Some idea of the difference between the police union and the Federation can can be seen from the first Federation conference in November 1919 which threw out a motion calling for the reinstatement of strikers and had all references to it struck from the minutes.[15] It became an offence against regulations for a policeman to call or attend 'any unauthorised meeting to discuss any matters concerning the force'.[16] The authorities solidified their victory over the union by buying loyalty through high pay rises.

A tradition was therefore established in the police force which is different from other industries. There are no unions, instead there are staff associations rigidly controlled from above. This has been imposed through a combination of force—the smashing of the strikes in 1918 and 1919—and persuasion which has taken a number of forms. The most important stems from the ideological conclusions police officers draw from their position in society, which we shall come too. However, it has also involved a good deal of bribery.

From back handers to back pockets

STUDY OVER time of the gap between police and workers' pay in Britain lends support to the idea that it is much more realistic to look upon the police as a body funded out of the profits created by workers, rather than a part of the working class which wins pay rises through its own struggles. In 1918 the differential in pay and conditions between police and workers had been allowed to decrease, the identity gap had narrowed and the British ruling class learned a lesson from that mistake.

It is only in times of rising class struggle that the need to buy off the police is absolutely obvious. So it is ironic that police forces do best in terms of wages and conditions when workers are fighting back. The police can gain from the struggles of the very workers who they are sent in to bludgeon.

In the earliest days of the police a policy decision was made that the level of police pay should not be set high enough to encourage army officers to apply for constables' posts.[17] Hours of duty were long, there were no agreed rest days and the turnover very high indeed.[18]

The situation changed partly because of some militancy amongst police themselves but often just the hint of rebellion was enough to bring about improvements. For example, in 1890 it took relatively mild industrial action by the police for them to gain extremely generous pension rights of three-fifths pay after 25 years service.[19] This was at a time when state pensions did not exist, and when occupational pensions were few and precious. In that year there were 1,028 strikes in Britain involving almost 393,000 workers, including 102 strikes by dockers and seafarers; 135 strikes in the cotton industry and 86 in coal mining.[20] During the next period of heightened workers' struggles the police gained the benefit of a guaranteed weekly rest day under the 1910 Act.

The gap between police and workers' pay narrowed during the First World War as leading trade unionists, with some notable rank and file exceptions, co-operated in the disciplining of labour as part of the war effort. After 1919, the police were bought off as much due to the threat of other workers as to their own efforts. The act which followed the work of the Desborough Committee increased pay dramatically and gave the police rent free accommodation, or a rent allowance, and the uncommon benefits of paid holidays, good pensions and guaranteed employment.[21]

Correspondingly, when the threat of working class action waned, so too did concern to secure police loyalty. When the miners were left to fight alone after the collapse of the Triple Alliance (of transport workers, railwaymen and miners) on 15 April 1921 the threat of united class action had been lessened. The ruling class was more confident. Police pay was actually cut by 2 percent in 1922.[22] However this was counted as a pensions contribution to sweeten the police during the 1926 General

Strike.[23] The importance of police loyalty was well enough understood by the ruling class. **Times** subscribers chipped in £240,000 to the Police Benevolent Fund. It was described by one chief inspector as a 'gargantuan tip ... from the upper classes'.[24]

After the defeat of the 1926 strike, the unions were seriously weakened for a decade. The gap between police and industrial workers' pay was eroded a little. There was a 5-10 percent wage cut in 1931.[25] Even the Police Federation echoed to some discontent. 'Open meetings were held all over the country with packed audiences of angry policemen'.[26] The National Unemployed Workers Movement responded with this leaflet in the early 1930s:

AN APPEAL TO THE POLICE

We, the unemployed workers are fighting for Bread, for Work, against the Means Test, for No More Economies.

You London Police know what the Government Economies have meant for us. As you walk the streets you see on every side of you the hunger, the misery, the bitter suffering forced on us and our families.

You also, do not escape. Today you are faced with another pay cut. *Despite promises made you, despite your Albert Hall protest, the document bluntly tells you that 'there is no alternative but to insist on the full police economies decided on last year.'*

Yet these same people rely on you to smash our fight against starvation.

They use you repeatedly to break up our Demonstrations. At Hyde Park on Thursday, they ordered you to attack us. *And they expect you to do the same again at Tuesday's Demonstration: To answer our cry for bread with batons.*

Why do it? Why act as thugs against hungry men and women? Why fight for the parasites who wallow in luxury while we, the masses, starve?

We call on you, help us in the fight to end the economies. Keep out of the way on Tuesday. Your own relatives are among our number. And only by supporting our fight against the economies can you defeat the cut in your own pay.

This is our call to you. But we also warn you. *If you attack us, we shall know how to defend ourselves, how to fight back.*

REMEMBER BIRKENHEAD
REMEMBER BELFAST (The London unemployed)[27]

The NUWM certainly had no illusions in the brutality or role of the police. Time and again the police had baton charged and mowed down marching ranks of the unemployed. The Glasgow NUWM fought police constraints on demonstrations in George Square, and in 1932 NUWM branches had to fight local police bans on demonstrations all over the country. In that year confrontations between police and unemployed demonstrators ranged from north to south.

For example, 10,000 people held a running fight with the police in North Shields as the marchers attempted to reach the Public Assistance Office. In the same year 15,000 battled at Bristol and,

> In Birkenhead following a peaceful protest of 10,000, police clubbed the dispersing crowds beating down men, women and children and then going on a night long rampage of terror, through the working class streets, breaking windows with their truncheons, dragging men from their beds and beating them bloody in front of their wives and children.[28]

However, the NUWM leaders calculated that loyalties might now be stretched and even broken. Unemployed workers' leader Wal Hannington repeated the appeal in a speech at Trafalgar Square. 'Let the working class in uniform and out of uniform stand together'.[29] He was arrested and charged with the serious crime of 'attempting to cause disaffection among members of the Metropolitan Police.'

But there is no real evidence of any link between police rebels and working class movements in the 1930s. The defensive struggles of the 1930s were different from the near revolutionary situation of 1918-1919 and throughout the inter war period, despite some cuts in police pay, it still remained at least 50 percent above average industrial earnings.[30]

Metropolitan Police Commissioner, Lord Trenchard, persuaded the Home Secretary to stop the Federation national committee from holding open meetings on the grounds that they were 'bad for discipline'.[31] The Police Federation could not possibly act as an independent union and the identity gap between workers and police was certainly not bridged in the inter war years.

During the post war boom of the late 1940s and early 1950s

picket line confrontations between police and workers were rare. The government was not prepared to be as generous towards the police as it had been after the First World War. The police did receive wage increases but whereas they had hoped for increases of between 33 percent and 55 percent from the Oaksey Committee in 1949, they were given 15 percent.[32] Not anticipating any problems, the government trusted the Police Federation with its own funds.

In the immediate post war period of full employment there were considerable problems of recruitment and retention of police. In 1949 there were 12,141 vacancies.[33] A review of police pay gave a generous 20 percent in 1950 to encourage recruitment and 9 percent in 1954.[34]

Tory prime minister Harold Macmillan's years of 'never had it so good' booming Britain were thinner for the police. A select committee in 1957-58 wasn't concerned about police vacancies but instead called for more mechanisation, civilianisation of the force, and that the police should claim 'a smaller share of the national manpower than hitherto.' By October 1959 the Police Federation were claiming that maximum and minimum pay for a constable were 1 percent and 28 percent respectively below average earnings in industry.[35]

There were eventually signs that the post war boom might not last forever and big demonstrations were organised by the Campaign for Nuclear Disarmament. The civil disobedience tactics of the Committee of 100 led to a nervousness: had the blue line been allowed to get too thin? Was that identity gap between police and workers too narrow? The Police Commission called for considerable pay increases for the police.[36]

The Police Federation employed a paid consultant, James Callaghan, subsequently Labour Prime Minister, who 'powerfully presented' their claim[37] which was met in full by a pay rise of £695-£910 for the constables on maxiumum pay.[38] The Commission argued the case for a pay formula designed to take into account the social and industrial changes since the war which had led to a worsening of the policeman's relative position. In 1962 the negotiating body signed an agreement providing for a biennial review of police pay.

The general objective was to link police pay to rises in the wages index and with the economic state of the country. Massive police recruitment followed this award. However the generosity of the pay arrangements were also accompanied by a reaffirmation that the police had no right to unionise. Section 47 of the 1964 Police Act stipulated that,

> a member of a police force shall not be a member of any trade union or of any association having for its objects or one of its objects, to control or influence the pay, pensions or conditions of service of any police force.[39]

A further old principle was reiterated in section 53 of the act, stating that it was a criminal offence,

> to cause disaffection among the police, rendering criminally liable 'any person who causes or attempts to cause, or does any act calculated to induce any member of the police force to withold his services or to commit breaches of discipline'.[40]

In the crisis ridden years of the last two decades police pay has shot up—rising 92.7 percent between 1978 and 1980 alone.[41]

What of police attitudes toward trade unionism? After the 1972 miners' strike a survey by Robert Reiner showed the average officer was, 'inclined to adopt a hostile stance towards trade unionism outside the force, and was prepared enthusiastically to support government attempts to curb union power with their help'.[42]

The Police Federation can undoubtedly exert pressure but it is no trade union. What trade union would have allowed its members to be completely excluded from all the employment protection legislation of the 1970s? The Federation operates like a company union, almost always doing what the bosses want. It is true that in 1977 there was a certain amount of campaigning within the police about trade union rights and the right to strike. But such dissidence was quickly quashed by a further bribe. In 1979 the Federation spent £21,000 on newpaper ads which were almost identical to those of the Conservative Party, which was fighting an election on a law and order campaign at the time.

Those who give the Police Federation some degree of 'worker credibility' should also remember that the Federation proposed, 'an immunity from prosecution for officers who wound or kill civilians in the course of their duty'.[43] It was the Police Federation that initially blocked the enforcement of the Scarman recommendation that racial discimination by police should be a disciplinary offence punishable by dismissal. Individual officers can make use of Federation funds to frighten people out of making complaints against them by threatening civil court action.

The representative organisations of the police, then, have been contained within the disciplined structure of the force and no independent trade union has developed. Indeed, one of the arguments used by the Federation itself to oppose the increasing recruitment of civilians into the police was that they might unionise, strike and undermine police effectiveness. Indeed, there has been successful unionisation amongst civilians whose recruitment as police back up has increased since 1970 to over 40,000. Police civilians in NALGO participated in the 1989 pay strike.

Shaped by the job

THE BEHAVIOUR and attitudes of groups in society are formed around their circumstances and experiences. Workers' attitudes are pulled in two main directions, among many others, by the pressures of capitalism. One—the pressure to compete for jobs, houses and other resources—can make them vulnerable to division, prey to racist and other reactionary ideas. At the same time, however, any successful fight for improved conditions has to be waged collectively. The circumstances of workers both makes such collective struggles possible—as they are grouped together in factories and offices—and very often points their anger against the boss, who they see attacking their living standards. This is why socialists look to workers as having the potential to fight for a better society.

The material conditions of the police are quite different. As we have seen, they get pay rises because of their importance in defending the existing order, not through struggling against the bosses. The establishment has also worked hard to cut off the path of collective resistance through breaking and banning police unions. Moreover, the very day to day experience of the police sets them not against the bosses, but against the working class and the oppressed.

At the broadest level, their job is to keep society running in its present form. This of course means doing whatever is demanded of them to help break strikes, as we have seen over the course of history.

More specifically, they are charged with defending property from those who are defined as being a threat to it. Therefore, to carry out the job given them, a police officer has to look with suspicion on anyone who fits the stereotype of the 'criminal'. To them it makes sense to be suspicious of working class communities. Workers have little and can be tempted to take back some of the riches held in the hands of others. Unemployed people, young people, black people—everyone who the police officer thinks should have little and may be tempted to break out from the bottom of society by taking more—are under suspicion for causing trouble, are pulled up for having cars or stereos that look as if they should be beyond their reach. Other tasks in defending the existing order reinforce stereotypes. We shall see, in particular, the way in which endemic police racism is constantly bolstered by the experience of implementing racist laws.

The police's job is to maintain a corrupt, unequal society; fulfilling that role means they can never be regarded simply as 'workers in uniform'. Like every other fraction of society, their position is determined by their relation to the rest of society. Workers, at least some of the time, and at least in objective terms, are impelled to stand together against the bosses. The police are compelled to stand together against the working class. As Leon Trotsky said,

> The fact that the policeman was originally recruited from [the ranks of]... workers is absolutely meaningless. Consciousness is determined by environment. The worker who becomes a policeman in the service of the capitalist state is a bourgeois cop, not a worker.[44]

The special position of the police starts to explain the role they have played in recent years, and the reactionary ideas and practices they have held towards society in general, towards women and against Black people in particular.

Chapter six

Post war policing and techno-cop

SINCE THE onset of economic crisis in early 1970s, the police have once more become more prominent in British politics. In the 1970s and 1980s there were revelations about the nasty workings of the secret state and violent confrontations on picket lines and streets.

Many people drew the conclusion that, under Thatcher in particular, Britain had become a 'police state'. Certainly, major changes in policing had occured since the end of the Second World War. By 1990 there were more police, with greater powers, more central organisation, greater riot training and more hardware than half a century earlier. This, however, does not make Britain a police state. What is a police state? Frederick Engels came up with one definition:

> The monstrous notion that anyone can place himself outside common law by maintaining an opinion. This is a pure police state.[1]

In a real police state, terror is the single most important method of control. This was not the case in Britain in the 1980s and 1990s. Most people were kept in line because they accepted the ideological fraud that the police were on hand to deal with crime. True, there is now a widespread perception of police corruption, but most people do not yet draw from this the conclusion that the police are the hired thugs of the wealthy. Keeping workers in subjegation, as the socialist Hal Draper argued, does not always,

> mean cowering under a whip—not necessarily and not usually... More generally it means also, in willing compliance, in passive acquiescence, or in ingrained dependence.

The ruling class relied in the first place on its economic pressure.[2]

The trouble with arguing the existence of a police state when there isn't one is that it both undermines workers' confidence, and draws our attention away from the real weaknesses in the workers' movement, such as cowardly union leadership.

In any case, state repression in Britain was certainly not a novel feature of Thatcher's reign. Rather, policing developments have run alongside changes in the economy, the level of class struggle and the effectiveness of other means of control.

During the post war boom there were few direct confrontations between the police and strikers or demonstrators. A schoolbook written in 1946 could refer to the policeman as the 'strong silent figure in the background.'[3] High profits were available to allow concessions and the army was often used as a strike breaking force. The troops used repeatedly by the Attlee Labour government did not require the same police protection as civilian scabs:

> The government decided on at least fourteen occasions between July 1945 and October 1951, to intervene in... disputes to keep essential supplies moving by drawing on its huge reserve of labour, the armed forces then swollen to nearly five million through conscription.[4]

Conscription continued long after the war ended, so there were two million men in the army alone. As the conflicts during this period involved dockers, unskilled and semi skilled labour (such as the Smithfield porters in 1947), the army could be used.[5] Profits were such that 'good will' could be secured through concessions and a more general feeling of security and increased prosperity spread over the working class as the boom proceeded. Under such conditions, the police had relatively little role to play in keeping the bosses' peace.

A stark, but rarely cited example of how little they cared what workers were up to, or what crimes were perpetrated against workers as long as they presented no threat, is the way in which the police didn't even patrol many council estates. These were regarded as private property.

Things, however, eventually changed. The 1957 Rent Act led to a whole series of confrontations between tenants and the police, including pitched battles to prevent evictions. Within two years of the act and faced with resistance from tenants, the following statement about council estates appeared in the Metropolitan Police Commissioner's report:

> These estates of varying sizes, many of which cover 100 acres with populations of several thousands *have been regarded as private in character, and hitherto have not normally been patrolled by the police*. During the course of the year proposals by the London County Council that police should afford a greater degree of supervision to their estates to preventing crime and disorderly behaviour were examined, and I have agreed that police will undertake to patrol those estates.[6]

This feigned concern for council tenants was more than a little hypocritical. In 1960 400 police were used in St Pancras to carry out evictions from council flats.

State forces were getting a little thin for the ruling class by the late 1950s and early 1960s. For example, in 1955 the strength of the Metropolitan Police, at 15,447, was three thousand less that it had been in 1912. The number of Specials and Reserves had fallen from 63,174 in 1954 to 49,328 in 1960.[7] Army numbers also were down following the ending of conscription from 2 million in 1947 to 250,000 in 1960.

Figure 5. Police, army and Specials numbers 1948-66

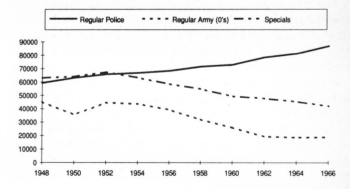

In any case, technological change made the possibility of using blacklegs from the army impractical for a whole range of occupations. In the summer of 1959 25,000 print workers in London went on strike and most of the 260 affected firms were picketted. Troops could certainly not replace these workers.[8]

Under the Wilson Labour Government of 1964-70 there was a dramatic increase in the number of regular police and both MI5 and Special Branch were used against workers.[9] There was a major reorganisation of the forces from 1964 onwards. The progressive amalgamation of forces to 47 increased effective centralisation and the power of the Chief Constables.

Table 5. Centralisation of forces, England and Wales.[10]

	Number of forces	Average size
1861	233	88
1921	183	332
1945	159	358
1965	120	704
1985	43	2771

This, together with many police being relieved of clerical and traffic jobs by civilians and traffic wardens, preceded the struggles of the 1970s.

Figure 6. Police civilians 1948-90.[11,12]

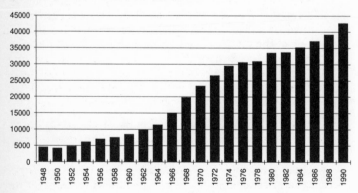

Saltley

THE UPTURN in class struggle in Britain during 1971-73 and in particular the miners' strike of 1972 made the ruling class extremely concerned about their forces, in spite of the stepping up of recruitment and reorganisation in the 1960s.

The organisation of rank and file miners in 1972 and their moblisation of other workers showed both the power that workers can wield, and the problems that the ruling class face when they are up against workers' organisation. Flying mass pickets were not the invention of Arthur Scargill or the Yorkshire miners in 1972. Back in the 1842 general strike, workers would march from town to town 'turning out' others. Even the police themselves used the mass flying picket in their 1919 strike[13] as did tailoring workers in Leeds in 1970.[14]

At Saltley coke depot in 1972 the thin blue line which protected the capitalist class from workers' collective power snapped. It was the last major source of coke during the strike and was successfully closed down by mass picketing. The word 'Saltley' has entered police short hand as a word meaning 'defeat'.

Initially there were a thousand lorries a day going in. For the strike to be successful the miners had to stop them. As the week progressed with mass pickets, fewer and fewer lorries were managing to leave the depot. Scargill appealed to Birmingham unions and things came to a head. In Scargill's words,

> Some of the lads... were a bit dispirited that no reinforcements were coming. And then over this hill came a banner... As far as the eye could see it was just a mass of people moving towards Saltley. There was a huge roar and from the other side of the hill they were coming the other way. They were coming from five directions... and our lads were just jumping up in the air with emotion...The roads all round the depot were jammed and the police with 800 men couldn't cope. 'Close the gates, close the gates' the crowd chanted.[15]

At 10.45 an official from the Gas Board closed the gates and Arthur Scargill borrowed the police public address system to disperse the crowd.

Three years later the special adviser to the chancellor of the exchequer, Brendon Sewill, wrote the following about Saltley:

At that time many of us in positions of influence looked into the abyss and saw only a few days away the possibility of the country being plunged into a state of chaos not so very far removed from that which might prevail after a minor nuclear attack. If that sounds dramatic—I need only say that with the prospect of the breakdown of power supplies, food supplies, sewerage, communication, effective government and law and order, it was the analogy that was being used at the time. Theirs is the power which exists to hold the country to ransom, it was the fear of that abyss which had important effects on subsequent policy.[16]

What had gone wrong for the ruling class? They had underestimated what rank and file workers' organisation could do. The question was asked: 'Could the army have been used as a back up to break the picket?' Home Secretary Reginald Maudling expressed ruling class hesitancy on this tactic by saying,

> one of my colleagues asked me afterwards why I had not sent the troops in to support the police, and I remember asking them one simple question. 'If they had been sent in, should they have gone in with their rifles loaded or unloaded?' Either course would have been disastrous.[17]

Troops were used again as scab labour in the early 1970s, in the dock strikes of 1972 and the Glasgow Fire Brigade strike of 1973 but it was recognised that such a policy had its limitations. In 1977 Lord Carrington produced a report for the use of the Conservative Party on the feasibility of using armed forces to break strikes. He took evidence from prominent businessmen and civil servants and,

> concluded that such a practice could not be adopted on any large scale for two reasons: first that Britain no longer had enough troops, and second, that it would permanently damage the fabric and practice of the country's politics.[18]

The Labour Government of 1974-79 seemed less nervous about using the troops and did use them extensively in the fireman's strike. Troops could not be used, however, when there was a bitter battle for union recognition at the small Grunwicks factory in West London in 1977. There was large rank and file support for the fight put up by a small group of Asian workers.

Although the ruling class had drawn the Saltley lesson the trade union leaders hadn't. For them the mass picket was not a way of winning the strike but just a demonstration of support. Roy Grantham, the general secretary of Apex, the union concerned, was to say that the aim of the mass picket was, 'to draw attention of the public authorities to the fact that we had a strike'.[19]

In fact the numbers at some of the mass pickets were sufficient, as they had been at Saltley, to stop the scab bus getting in. But the union leadership led the pickets away from Grunwicks and stopped subsequent attempts to build effective mass pickets. The actions of the union leaders undermined the powerful unity of black and white workers that could have won that struggle.

The Labour government which came to power on the backs of the miners' struggle in 1974 also increased police numbers substantially and began the revision of police strategy that followed the defeat at Saltley.

Figure 7. Police numbers under Labour and Tories.

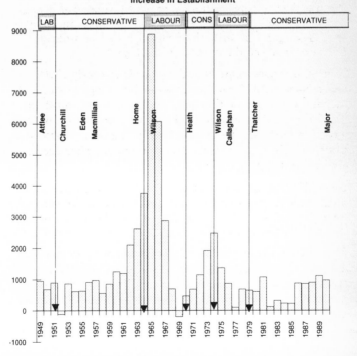

Increase in Establishment

The Ridley Report

WORLD RECESSION in the late 1970s meant that curtailing the power of organised labour and attempting to force down real wages to preserve profits became crucial to the bosses. But how to do it presented a dilemma. Massive unemployment was not having the disciplining effect that was anticipated and workers put up some tough defensive fights. In May 1978 a key Tory Party strategy document was leaked. It classified industries into three categories of vulnerability to strike action. This Ridley Report,

> rejected proposals to make strikes illegal and any idea of having a strike breaking corps of volunteers to run mines, trains or power stations. In strikes in industries which 'have the nation by the jugular vein', it argued 'the only feasible option is to pay up' ... the group also put forward proposals to fragment state industries, set them inflexible targets and *form a large mobile squad of anti picket police*.[20]

One of the tests for such a force came in 1983 when Eddie Shah launched an attack against print workers. A mass picket was called to stop scab work coming out of his Warrington plant. There were 4,000 on the biggest overnight picket.[21] It was just few enough for the police to try out their riot squads and techniques. In the early hours of the morning it was like a mediaeval battle scene with broken heads and other injuries. The **Financial Times** was well satisfied and reported the following day:

> the police tactics at Warrington ... show clearly that they had learnt the hard lesson of mass picketting over the past ten years... [Unlike the case with] the miners at Saltley gates... where perhaps 15,000 pickets led a completely overwhelmed police contingent to order the shutting of the picketed coke depot.[22]

The role of the police came into sharp focus in the miners' strike of 1984-85. There was a far bigger police mobilisation than there had been in the 1972 and 1974 strikes. Mobile riot squads and large numbers of police were used to break the pickets with a major confrontation at the strategic Orgreave coking plant. The Tories harked back again to the lessons of Saltley. The Home Secretary told the 1986 Tory Conference:

Years ago the miners succeeded in sweeping the police aside and shutting down the industry by force at Saltley coke works, but this time the police held their line.[23]

But it wasn't just the state forces that beat the miners in 1984-5. There was also a clamp down at the local level of the union on rank and file control.

More important was the unwillingness of the TUC to mobilise action in support. Militants recognised steel production was the Tories' vulnerable point and that stopping the Orgreave coking plant was crucial to winning the struggle. The union bureaucracies at local and national level did not agree and the rank and file organisation wasn't there to make the picket massive enough. The outcome was a police-controlled blood bath instead of another Saltley. The miners' defeat at Orgreave was wrongly attributed just to the police strength and violence. It was true that the miners of 1984-85 faced a much harder force than in 1972 or 1974. But it was wrong to imply that the police alone had beaten them.

What changes have taken place? The police have drawn heavily on the experience of colonial policing in the 1950s and 1960s. Baton rounds were developed in Hong Kong. CS gas and water cannon were first used in Cyprus.[24] In the early 1960s Hong Kong police placed heavy emphasis on riot training with its Police Training Contingent which was, 'a police reserve unit... available for sending men to any outbreak of public disorder'.[25]

The riot squads in mainland Britain followed a similar pattern. First came the Special Patrol Group and then the Police Support Units which consisted of,

> squads of 23 police officers; 2 sections of ten constables each under the control of a sergeant with an inspector in command. In general each police division provides a minimum of one PSU; this does not operate as a group locally, but trains periodically so as to be ready when called for active service on 'foreign territory'. Their deployment is effectively controlled by the President of the Association of Chief Police Officers.[26]

By 1987 all recruits were receiving public order training at the Police Holding and Training Centres at Hounslow and Greenwich.[27] The PSUs received extra riot training:

It was the PSUs which were the first to be equipped with the new riot gear, with CS gas and plastic bullets. With 416 police support units drawn from all the 43 police forces in England and Wales they furnished a riot force of specially trained officers 10,000 strong available for services anywhere in Britain. To this must be added the numerically smaller elite shock troops of the Special Patrol Group and other comparable regional formations.[28]

The terror policing experience of Northern Ireland was available for the mainland forces. The rhythmic drumming on the riot shields and the very appearance of marching riot squads in full gear stimulates fear. In a sick comment on police 'excesses' allowed under such conditions, a Chief Inspector said:

> If you do a policeman's job you are bound to know all the dirty tricks of the trade... I'm sure it goes on... You've got a dog job to do, if you've got a dog you've got to give it a lump of sugar now and then... It's a bit like generals turning a blind eye to raping and pillaging in war time.[29]

Police can set up four types of cordons and then open up to let in snatch squads. Observers from a vantage point look out not only for those who are particularly aggressive but for those who might be 'outsiders'. Cordons, wedges, formations, baton charges and mounted police charges have been developed over the years. Details of riot tactics and training are to be found in the Public Order Manual of Tactical Options.[30]

Technological development is not peculiar to the British police, it has been happening to police forces on a world scale. The riot police the world over are almost indistinguishable in their gear:

> In 1975 for example the United States Agency for International Development estimated that over one million foreign policemen had received some training or supplies through its public safety programme... not only in routine police matters but also in paramilitary techniques and counter insurgency.[31]

So similar is international riot policing that when film makers in the US looked for props for a film about Poland, they were to hand locally. One scene involved the Polish Zomo (riot police) ramming a tank into the main gate of the Wjeclk mine:

The Zomo were played by the National Guard whose standard issue tank has a profile conveniently similar to the Warsaw Pact tank... [These] were last mobilised to break a sit-in strike at a local factory.[32]

Police riot technology has also become international business. British firms have a big share of the world market. Britain has become a world 'brand leader' in riot control weapons, exporting them worldwide. Plastic bullets are made by Pains-Wessex Schermuly of Salisbury. Countries to which the bullets have been exported include Spain, Portugal, South Africa and Iran under the Shah.[33] The Police Scientific Development Board Equipment Laboratory has developed a strobe gun operating at five flickers per second and designed to cause a mild form of epilepsy. Another weapon of coercion, vomit gas, was developed at the government chemical warfare establishment at Porton Down.[34]

Plastic bullets sound like light and vaguely unpleasant toys. In fact they are 10 cm long, 2.5 cm wide and fire at between 130 and 170 km/h.[35] Between April 1972 and August 1981 13 people, six of them children were killed by rubber and plastic bullets in Northern Ireland. Many more suffered horrific injuries, including blindness in one or both eyes.[36]

Riot control equipment and techniques are sophisticated in that they aim for controlled terror. They are designed to be 'slightly less than lethal'. If they kill, it appears to be 'as if by accident'. The thinking behind riot technology is that,

> It is preferred that onlookers do not get the impression that the police are using excessive force or that the weapon has an especially injurious effect on the target individuals. Here again, a flow of blood or similar dramatic effects are to be avoided.[37]

But each terror technique has its limitations. If the police wear heavy equipment to protect themselves, then their movements are impeded. People can disrupt the supplies to the water cannon which proved not very mobile and of limited use in Northern Ireland. CS gas blew back into the soldiers' faces and vinegar was found to be a useful antidote to the worst effects. Furthermore, when it comes to confrontations, the ruling class does not always dare to use all the technology at its disposal.

In the fearful recognition of the arrival of the 'techno cop' it is often forgotten that during the 1984 miners' strike in Britain the police had plastic bullets and tear gas. They did not use them on miners' pickets line as they had used them against inner city youth in 1981 for fear of provoking wider, more powerful workers' struggles. It is not even true that the police could simply have moved into Saltley in 1972 with 3,000 riot police, CS gas, plastic bullets, kept the gates open and finished the strike. The expert on counter insurgency, Richard Clutterbuck, said of Saltley:

> The police could without question, have kept the road open, and strictly it was their duty to do so. They could have done this by deploying say 3,000 instead of 800... and if necessary by using water cannon, tear gas or rubber bullets. Any of these things, however would have unleashed far greater violence and sacrificed public sympathy.[38]

The strength and numbers of organised workers can undermine the effectiveness of any technology the state can produce. Workers make the equipment and can take it back. For example, South Korean demonstrators were able to get some of the police's riot gear and wear it themselves. But more important are sheer numbers. In the last resort all riot training and technology, however sophisticated, depends on the assumption that the police are outnumbered, but not massively so.

Despite the new technology, the police often rely on time tested allies, the dog and the horse. As the Duke of Wellington remarked in the nineteenth century,

> It is much more desirable to employ the cavalry for the purpose of police than infantry, for the reason cavalry inspires more terror at the same time that it does less mischief.[39]

But when horses were more familiar workers would cut their reins and striking French abattoir workers had no scruples about cutting the horses' throats.

The police now have greater legal powers in addition to more access to technology. The 1984 Police and Criminal Evidence Act and the Public Order Act of 1986 were brought in after the 1981 riots and the miners' strike. The Police and Criminal Evidence Act allows the police 96 hours detention without coming to court, extended powers of stop and search, intimate body searches, and changed questioning procedures making forced confessions easier.[40] The Public Order Act significantly increases police powers to control demonstrations, particularly 'static demonstrations', or mass pickets. The act includes sections requiring seven days notice to be given of demonstrations and creates an offence of 'failing to comply with police directions' which enables police to inflict harsher penalities on organisers. The act contains three newly worded collective offences: riot, violent disorder and affray which are easier to prove and which, respectively, carry sentences of ten, five and three years imprisonment. However police powers cannot destroy opposition by themselves:

> The law is designed to handle individuals or small groups. It can be overwhelmed by masses. It can crush even the bravest individual because it has a massive apparatus of courts, police and prisons. But these cannot cope with thousands or millions of workers. We are simply too many for them.[41]

Policing the News International dispute at Wapping in 1986-7 was a very expensive business. Three hundred officers were regularly used per day; over 1,000 were used on 12 occasions.[42] 1,375 arrests were made at Wapping and mounted police were engaged there on 263 occasions, such was the importance to British capital of Murdoch's union smashing efforts. The police used the practised tactics of mounted police charges, snatch squads and general terror.

The tragedy was that, following the miners' strike and the defeat of the printers, many drew the conclusion that the state couldn't be beaten. They feared that the new technology and the ease of storing information had created the all powerful, all seeing Big Brother state.

It is true that an enormous amount of data is housed in a specially fortified building in Hendon, north London. A new national police computer, PNC2, was started up there in December 1991. It stores information on over 5 million people. The computer notes which people on the criminal list have been tested HIV positive. 125,000 transactions can be performed per day.

The car information on the old PNC proved a nuisance to the miners' pickets. Telephone tapping also caused nervousness and alarm. But even now phone tapping is very inefficient. Telephone tapping is useless against mass organisation if day to day control rests in the hands of the rank and file where messages can be passed by word of mouth or where telephone engineers can themselves be brought into the struggle. This dependence on workers was illustrated by the fight by the carefully vetted telephone spies at GCHQ to preserve their union.

Technology has also increased the ease with which workers can communicate and organise. In the mass picketing of the 1842 strike, it was sometimes a ten mile walk to turn out factories in other towns.

With or without taps, nineteenth century workers had no telephones for communication, no loud hailers or microphones to address meetings. Leaflets often had to be written and duplicated by hand. Typewriters and duplicators were recognised as potential workers' weapons and were smashed up. In 1849 Marx published a statement by Engels in which it was pointed out that muzzling the oppressed class must also involve the direct suppression where possible of the 'the cost free literature and give-away leaflet'.[43]

The production of political street literature is much easier today and many workers have access to photo copying and duplicating technology. For example, at the end of May 1989 in China, when students and workers in their hundreds of thousands controlled central Beijing,

> On the streets elsewhere in the city people cluster round wall posters. Many of these are produced by photocopiers... Electronics are making life easier for protest organisers not least because the advent of direct dial phones and fax machines seriously undermines government attempts to block communications by putting bans on the content and distribution of newspapers, magazines and radio broadcasts.[44]

1990 saw the confrontation between police and poll tax demonstrators in Trafalgar Square. The police's role as a violent force defending the ruling class was clear. Even in this campaign it was the failure of Labour politicians and councils to organise around the anti poll tax anger that inhibited the growth of the campaign rather than any action by the police.

The term 'police state' implies difficulties of organisation and extensive spy networks which do not exist in Britain. There is no necessity for undercover organisation. The relative freedom of the press, freedom of association, freedom to form working class organisations are not imaginary but real freedoms which are of fundamental importance to socialists because they make organisation so much easier. The most important democratic right the working class has is the ability to form its own independent organisations. Whilst some of these are under attack and must be defended, they are essentially intact.

Certainly under the Tories there has been less good will and more force and fraud, but Britain remains a parliamentary democracy and the ruling class depends far more on the union bureaucrats and Labour leaders to reconcile the antagonism of class interests than on the police to win by exertion of terror.

Open discussion, disagreement, freedom to assemble and opposition parties and press are permitted in a capitalist parliamentary democracy because they are part of the fraud that workers actually have some say in controlling the system.

Chapter seven

Police and the right

JUST HOW strong are the police? Theories abound which describe them as increasingly powerful. Some of these even take police coercion as evidence of 'creeping fascism.' This notion became quite popular in Labour Party circles during the 1980s.

Sure, there are fascists and ex-fascists in the Tory party, and not a few among the ranks of the police. But Britain in the 1980s and early 1990s was a million miles away from fascism—a system under which every form of workers' resistance and organisation is annihalated.

It is true, however, that the police establishment works in league with many anti-democratic individuals and organisations. They even weaken democracy themselves through their actions. And, they have a long record of defending fascists.

Defending the fascists

IN THE 1930s the police's defence of Sir Oswald Mosley's British Union of Fascists was in stark contrast to its record of assaults on unemployment demonstrations:

> In so far as the Metropolitan and provincial forces ever intervened at fascist demonstrations, they invariably did so to protect the fascists from the fury of the crowd (which had already been provoked by Blackshirt violence) or to arrest anti fascist counter demonstrators. Whenever the Fascist Defence Force was powerful enough to handle interrupters with their own peculiar savagery, the police were usually content to preserve a benevolent neutrality.[1]

The Public Order Act of 1936, passed ostensibly to curtail the activities of the fascists, was subsequently used much more frequently against the left. The fascists were stopped from gaining control of the streets in the East End of London, but in spite of the efforts of the police, not because of them. Opposition to fascist marches culminated in the battle of Cable Street on 4 October 1936:

> The anti-fascists in the area were opposed by 6,000 constables and the whole of the Mounted Division ... it required more than a dozen baton charges by hundreds of police to breach the barricades which anti-fascists had set up in Cable Steet... Support for Mosley cost nearly 100 policemen serious injury, and as a result of the determined opposition of anti fascists, many hundreds of whom had been severely injured by baton and horse charges, the Commissioner abandoned the march.[2]

With the rise of the National Front in the 1970s, the police brutalised the Nazis' opponents, most notably after the fascists were successfully driven from the streets of Lewisham, south London in 1977 and at Southall in 1979 when anti fascist and Socialist Workers Party member Blair Peach was killed by the police.

The police's attitude of defending fascists, while seeing their opponents as a greater threat to public order, was summed up in a pocket book produced by the **Police Review** in 1978:

> The National Front ... preach Britain for the British... All of their meetings are well run and orderly, but their nature and venue frequently provoke trouble. National Front supporters have been described as the type of person who lives on a decent council estate, or his own small home which he has saved hard to buy, who sees coloured people taking over the area in which he lives and getting the benefits which he should get.
>
> The Socialist Workers Party is led by middle class revolutionaries ... Their enemy is capitalism and the establishment, and their aim is the destruction of existing society.[3]

The hidden hand

IF THE LEFT and the unions don't face physical annihilation by the police, have they been rendered impotent by the activities of the 'secret state'?

The term 'secret police' is used in Britain to mean MI5, MI6 and the Special Branch. They are neither as effective nor as secret in Britain as the right or left often think. But they can be both vicious and dangerous.

MI6 was set up to be responsible for espionage abroad, MI5 with internal spies. Both are sections of Military Intelligence and tend to draw their recruits from public schools and in the old days from 'Indian colonial police of quite extraordinary stupidity'. Particular London clubs were recruiting grounds for MI6.[4] The office jobs go to women of good family connections; 'mainly daughters of society and service families'.[5]

Often MI6 is hopelessly ineffective. The government Franks Report on the Falklands War said at the time that, 'The press seemed better informed of Argentina than the intelligence agency.'[6] More generally:

> The intelligence that the world's secret services produce is unverifiable gossip or economic analysis culled from freely available papers and specialist journals. Even when secret services do produce vital information, it is only used when it conforms to the political prejudices of the ruling class.[7]

Like other secret services, MI6 goes in for destabilising regimes which are deemed unsatisfactory to British ruling class interests. The politics are conspiratorial and can include any number of illegal activities. MI6 plotted to assassinate Egypt's Colonel Nasser in 1956.[8]

The secret services are not some monolithic secret state but are themselves riven with feuds and antagonisms. Classic, but not clear, are the conflicts between MI5, MI6, Special Branch and Military Intelligence in Northern Ireland.[9] Conflicts have also been reported between the French and British secret services. The French secret service left a bomb in the gardens of the French Embassy in London during President Mitterrand's visit to hit back at the British secret service.[10]

Such feuding between different sets of spies led one spy

author to explain the function of the secret service in the following manner:

> The decisive reason for the existence and endless proliferation of the KGB, SIS and the rest is to spy on each other. The intelligence agencies of the world have become a kind of mutual insurance society to keep each other in business.[11]

The legal existence of MI5 was denied for years though it dates back to 1909, the beginning of the Great Unrest. Today it is supposed to operate 'within a framework welded into legislation' but there is no real external accountability.[12] Labour prime minister James Callaghan once burbled the excuse:

> I am not sure what its accountability to parliament is... I am going to give you a very unsatisfactory answer. I do not know... I am very, very mixed up about this. I do not think I can help you much on this.[13]

MI5 has a special section called AIA (Technical Operations) whose only work is breaking and entering private property. Former agent Cathy Massiter revealed her work had,

> consisted of surveilling CND members and she talked of burglaries of trade union leaders' houses, and the many pointless exercises of placing bugs in houses which appeared to represent a threat to paranoid members of the right wing establishment.[14]

The murder of 78 year old anti-nuclear activist Hilda Murrell in 1984 showed the deadly serious side of MI5 as the killing had all the hallmarks of a botched MI5 job.[15]

During Harold Wilson's government in the 1960s there are claimed to have been about 30 MI5 officers who went quite berserk and were convinced that there was a Communist cell at 10 Downing Street and that Hugh Gaitskell had been poisoned by tea and biscuits at the Soviet Embassy to make way for the 'red' Harold Wilson.[16] This sort of idiocy is detailed in Peter Wright's bestselling book **Spycatcher** which the British government spent a million pounds trying to get blocked by the courts.

The paranoic plots of MI5 against Harold Wilson's Government are trivial compared with the secret state's operations in

Northern Ireland. 'Shoot to kill' revelations and the Gibraltar killings in 1988 have shown the murderous nature of secret operations. There are other side effects to their intrigues. For example, for 20 years the police in Northern Ireland were aware that boys at Kincora children's home were being used as prostitutes by Tara, an extreme Unionist sect. But nothing was done to protect those children, probably because MI5 wanted to be able to use this knowledge in its own intrigues.[17]

MI5 have no legal special powers in Britain, so many of the open arrests and searches are carried out for them by Special Branch. For example, the search of the Glasgow BBC offices after revelations about the secret £500 million expenditure on the spy satellite Zircon was carried out by Special Branch working with MI5.

The Special Branch were set up before MI5 in the nineteenth century, as the Irish Special Branch, officially to combat Fenian bombings. The word 'Irish' was dropped from the title in 1888.[18] An Irish section was retained, but activities were extended to cover other groups identified as the internal enemy. After the First World War their job was to 'save England from "Red" machinations'.[19]

A police history in the 1950's stated that the Special Branch was, 'the political police for the whole country. It aims at collecting information about 'undesirable' political persons and movements.'[20]

But who are these undesirables? In 1963 the definition of subversion, according to Lord Denning, included those activities which 'contemplate by unlawful means the overthrow of government'. Merlyn Rees in 1978 described subversives as those *he* thought were causing a problem for the state. Under Margaret Thatcher the definition was extended: a subversive was someone who,

> Is or has recently been a member of a Communist or Fascist organisation or subversive group acknowledged to be such by the minister, whose aims are to undermine or overthrow parliamentary democracy in the United Kingdom by political, industrial, or violent means... Is or has recently been sympathetic to or associated with members or sympathisers of such organisations or groups in such a way as to raise reasonable doubts about his reliability. Is

susceptible to pressure from such organisations or groups.[21]

Because recruitment to MI5 tends to be of paranoic right wingers many groups which would be horrified at the idea of overthrowing the state are included. Edward Heath, Tory prime minister from 1970 to 1974, said that some people in the security services 'talked the most ridiculous nonsense' and seemed to want to pursue **Daily Mirror** readers.[22] One former Chief Constable of the York, North and East Riding police said,

> I would say anyone who's decrying marriage, family life, trying to break that up, pushing drugs, advocating the acceptance of certain drugs, homosexuality, indiscipline in schools, weak penalties for anti-social crimes... a whole gamut of things that could be pecking away at the foundations of our society... if a chap doesn't like a file being kept on him... that's just the kind of chap we should be keeping files on.[23]

Another, more rational top officer, John Alderson, admitted that: 'Much of the information is valid intelligence. A substantial proportion is unchecked bunkum.'[24] When he became Chief Constable of Devon and Cornwall in 1982, he found that, 'Several hundred files had accumulated over the years, and a senior police officer stated that only 20 were worth preserving.'[25]

Special Branch look for conspiracies everywhere. They sometimes pay informers and occasionally get information from people arrested for non political offences by offering to drop charges in exchange for co-operation. Undercover work is, 'mainly undertaken by the other intelligence agencies... The numbers involved at any moment are quite small, usually not more than twenty or thirty officers'.[26] These are most likely to operate in 'ad hoc campaigns where few of the people know each other'.[27]

But much more important than undercover surveillance is the information gathering. They collect from left wing newspapers, petitions, address books, attendances at meeting and have extensive files on very large numbers of people. These files may be used for vetting juries, particularly in political trials.

They have been effective in harassing individual immigrants or helping in the victimisation of industrial militants. According to John Alderson, the Special Branch were responsible for building up a file on any significant industrial dispute in their area whether a criminal offence had been committed or not. Whenever MI5 open a file on somebody, a note is sent to Special Branch.[28]

To get the Special Branch in perspective it has been estimated to have about 2,000 officers, 25 civilian staff and a nominal budget of about £25 million per year with departments in all provincial police forces.[29] Special Branch's main difficulty, however, is that it is geared up to subverting small, secretive organisations. Unfortunately for them, most successful organisations in a country such as Britain build on as wide and as open a basis as possible.

Private eyes

THE OFFICIAL police are often helped in gathering information on industrial disputes and militants by an array of private security firms, many of which have political origins. For example, Securicor was set up in 1935 to,

> give additional security to the residents of the penthouses in London's Park Lane area...
> Unemployment was high, as was the incidence of serious public order disturbances triggered off largely by the antics of Oswald Mosley's British Union of Fascists. The private police were in effect a precautionary measure to protect the penthouse set should disturbances spill over from their focus in London's East End ... George Lansbury linked them with Mosley's militaristic formations and his fascist protection squads, for Lansbury as for many others, the private police were seen as the first halting steps towards fascism.[30]

Securicor was disbanded during the Second World War, presumably because of suspicions of links with fascism.[31]

Private security firms flourished in the post war period. In June 1973 a firm called Complete Security Services Ltd., then a subsidiary of Securicor, sent out a circular offering employers a man 'planted among your employees to report on untoward behaviour and to undertake research into the background and antecendents of workers.'[32] The declarations of political neutrality of security companies are as nonsensical as similar claims made by the regular police. These security firms,

> exist to make a profit themselves as well as to guard, and help maximise others' profits. The striker, the industrial spy and the radical trade union activists on the shop floor are the natural enemy of the private police, for by stopping production they endanger profits. It is therefore their commercial role which takes them to the centre of the political arena.[33]

The Economic League has similar links with the police and is more important in victimising activists. It was set up by group of businessmen in 1919 when fear of revolution was at its height. Its professed aim was:

> To assist the development of a widespread understanding of the value and importance of profitable industry and commerce within the UK mixed economy. To fight subversion and to keep members informed of the activities of those who are hostile to productive enterprise in industry and commerce.[34]

As the first part of the aim is continually being met by the media and television today it is the latter activity of vetting which has encouraged subscriptions to the League from some 2,000 companies.[35] The aim of its founder, Sir Reginald 'Blinker' Hall, was to form a 'new intelligence service to deal with 'Labour unrest, revolutionary matters, aliens and counter espionage' which would be 'independent from government.'[36]

In 1987 the TV programme World in Action filmed Alan Harvey, then Assistant Director of the League's North East region, explaining how it received information from the police. The formal links with Special Branch,

> include providing it with their press-cutting service. The League has also supplied full time officials to lecture on training courses for military and Special Branch officers, usually on the role of political and industrial subversion in society... Similar lectures have been given by League officials at joint intelligence courses organised by MI5.[37]

Information flows both ways. In 1978 the London region of the League had 'four men who had professional security or police backgrounds working in the research department'.[38] Its files are massive, containing an estimated 40,000 names. The League's definition of subversive is as generous as that of MI5 and Special Branch. The list of groups indicate the extreme right wing nature of the organisation. But, nonsensical though it may be, inclusion in the lists can mean the loss of jobs. Richard Brett, Director of the North West Region in 1985-88, said the register, otherwise known as the blacklist, is a shambles.[39]

Some idea of the bias may be gained from the case of Andrew Jeffrey who prepared a report investigating the activities of the far right in his local area. The League did not use Jeffrey's work as a source of information on the right but instead it blacklisted him.[40] Perhaps the most unpleasant information given by a whistle blower on the League was that,

> Not all trade unionists, however, are opposed to the League. Officials say that many trade unions actually tolerate the organisation 'because they don't want political extremists anymore than the companies do... And we do actually have a speaker from a trade union once a year'.[41]

There is one amusing aspect of the fact that the operations of the Economic League and Special Branch and MI5 run so closely together. As one League officer said,

> who knows... we may have the names of Special Branch infiltrators on our files who signed attendance sheets at meetings.[42]

Awareness of the political activities of MI6, MI5, Special Branch, security companies and the Economic League should be tempered with the knowledge that they are not all seeing nor all powerful and, like most secret services, face the problem of being flooded by out of date and useless information.

Even under highly repressive conditions, in which the secret police assume greater importance in harassing and blocking opposition, outbreaks of mass struggle have very often made them irrelevant. All the Tsar's secret police were not able to stop the Russian Revolution. Nor did the Iranian secret police, the Savak, protect the Shah or the Stasi prevent the overthrow of the East German government.

The existence and activities of the secret police in Britain make a sham of the claim that we live in an unfettered demo-cracy. Their activities in Northern Ireland have very often been murderous. They are not in general, however, the biggest obstacle to workers' resistance and organisation.

—

Chapter eight
Police and racism

RACISM IS institutionalised in the police force, not just an unpleasant characteristic of individual policemen. It exists at every level of the force. Inspector Peter Johnson, who referred to black people as 'nig-nogs' at a 1984 Police Federation meeting, was no ordinary officer. He had served on a Home Office Working Party on Race Relations, the National Police Training Council, the European Police Executive, and has been the Chair of the Inspectors' Branch of the Federation.[1] The report of the Chief Constable of Merseyside to the Scarman Commission in 1981 was packed with assertions about minorities in Liverpool, ranging from accusations against the Irish, Jews and Blacks and associating them with 'mugging', prostitution and drugs.[2]

Similar slurs were made by Superintendent John Ellis in Leeds in 1987. He said that in the Chapeltown area, 'there are 15,000 West Indians living in the locality... They create all sorts of problems... Drugs... Prostitution, brothels and vice'.[3] The operational chief of the Metropolitan Police Number 6 Area in West London said that street signs for the 1986 Notting Hill Carnival should read 'Coons Go Home'.[4]

London's chief constable asked the Policy Studies Institute in 1979 to produce a study of the 'relations between the Metropolitan Police and the community it serves'. The report refers to some senior officers who,

> undoubtedly overlooked racialism or racial prejudice when it was manifest, or participated in racialist talk themselves... It was a chief inspector who worked himself up into a frenzy of hatred against black people and orchestrated a session of absurd racialist talk with a large group of PCs in the canteen.[5]

The racism of what is termed 'canteen culture' is well documented (it is common for officers to spend a total of three hours or more in the canteen out of an eight hour shift).[6] During the PSI research in January 1981 there was a devastating fire at a birthday party in Deptford which killed 13 young black people. One constable asked the researcher: 'How many of these niggers actually fried in this barbeque at Deptford then?'[7]

The police wouldn't investigate the possiblity that the fire was a racist arson attack. Instead they harrassed the youngsters still under shock from the fire in an attempt to show that it had been started by Black party goers. The Black Day of Action in protest involved some 15,000 people and a confrontation with the police. The day after the demonstration 'racialist comments abounded' according to the researcher and one officer described the march as 'hundreds of rampaging niggers'.[8]

The police establishment occasionally makes empty promises about combatting racism in the force, but this is always seen as a problem of individual officers. Lord Scarman, who rejected any idea of *institutionalised* police racism, said:

> I have seen that immense trouble has been taken since 1981 to supervise the attitudes and reactions of police recruits going through their initial training. Those who show signs of racial prejudice will either have it eradicated by training, advice or leadership or they will go.[9]

The story of John Fernandes and Hendon Police College shows Scarman to have been wrong. After the 1981 riots a multicultural unit was set up at the college with a black lecturer, John Fernandes, as its head. He designed a course to combat racism amongst the cadets, which was stopped by the chief officer, Commander Wells. John Fernandes gave examples of cadets' essays to the media in order to establish the necessity of the course. They included such comments as:

> 'Blacks in Britain are a pest ... spooning off the state ... they are by nature unintelligent.' ... 'They must fall in line under white British dictators' ... 'They go out with white women and take white men's jobs' ... 'Can a shotgun blast a black man to pieces at 12 yards?' ... 'Do black people burn better with oil or petrol?'... Many said that in future lessons they would like to know more about the NF.[10]

John Fernandes was sacked for this exposure. The cadets remained in the force and Commander Wells was subsequently promoted to the post of Deputy Assistant Commissioner.

However, police racism does not arise simply because racists are recruited into the force. Police practice and culture increase racism.[11] Group attitudes within the police force are such as to reinforce racist attitudes where they exist among recruits and create them where they are lacking. The Policy Studies Institute noted,

> there can be few other groups in which it is normal, automatic, and habitual to refer to black people as 'coons', 'niggers' and so on... a woman detective constable... told [the researcher]... that before she joined she used to wince when people used words like 'coon', 'wog', and 'nigger'; she had pledged to herself that she would never use such terms. She pointed out that the habitual use of words like these, as part of police jargon, was uniform throughout the Force, and admitted that she herself now said 'spade' and 'spook' constantly, though she couldn't explain why.[12]

One measure of the racism within the police force is given by the very low number of Black officers. They made up only 1 percent of police officers in England and Wales in 1989, compared with about 4 percent of the economically active population.[13] It's worth examining the recruitment statistics a little more closely.

Table 6. Ethnic minority recruits and strength, England and Wales.[14]

Year	Recruits	Total strength
1986	239	1,232
1987	396	1,526
1988	251	1,623
Total	886	actual increase 391

Table 6 indicates a rapid turnover of those Blacks who are recruited. In 1989, while 35 blacks joined the Metropolitan Police, 26 left.[15]

Details of the kind of racial abuse which Black recruits have to tolerate was illustrated in the case of PC Surinder Singh.[16] A year-long industrial tribunal upheld his allegation that his promotion in the force had been thwarted by racial disrimination. The snapshot given of the force was one of crude racism with all the terms of abuse being used against Black recruits. Clearly when Black people join the police they either accommodate to the racism or get out.

The low numbers of ethnic minority recruits is a clear sign and a symptom of racism, but not its cause. Across England and Wales even the police civilians and traffic wardens are almost exclusively White, making up 99.1 percent and 98.2 percent respectively of the forces outside London in 1989. In the Metropolitan Police, however, 13 percent of civilians and 9 percent of traffic wardens are classified as Asian or Afro-Caribean.[17] Yet this factor, which means the London police have to work alongside Black people, has not diminished their racism by one jot.

Among groups of predominantly White workers, it is often common to find a good deal of racism. But even here, arguments from anti-racists and the experience of fighting against the boss can undermine these ideas. With the police it is different. Racism is necessary for the job. It arises out the divisive function they perform. The police rarely experience collective struggle which can break down racial prejudice. Indeed when the police are engaged in group activities, it is often in conflict situations which increase racist attitudes.

An increase in the recruitment of Black police will not end police racism. It was a policy throughout British colonial history to recruit Black constables into the colonial police and large-scale Black recruitment into the American police has not ended police racism there.

Part of the job

THE POLICE don't just use racist language and abuse, they operate laws in a racist manner. For example, the police harassment of young Blacks is widespread. In the 1970s much of this was carried out under the 'sus' offence of the 1824 Vagrancy Act. 'Sus' simply involved 'being a suspected person loitering with intent' and could be used against anyone who had not committed any offence. Before the law was repealed, Metropolitan Police statistics showed that blacks were 15 times more likely than whites to be arrested for 'sus'.[18]

Despite the repeal of the 'sus' laws, the 1984 Police Act leaves the police with even greater powers to stop and search. These powers are consistently operated in a racist fashion, as is shown by the following table:

Table 7. Number of times stopped by police on foot or in vehicle in last year, men, 15-24 years[19]

	Whites	West Indians	Asians
% stopped	44	63	18
Mean number of stops among those stopped	2.58	4.10	2.09

Across all age groups the percentage of people who have been stopped by the police when on foot is nearly four times as high among West Indians as among whites. It is even more striking when the statisics are broken down to look at particular age groups being stopped in cars. For West Indian youths who have been stopped at all, the mean number of stops is 5.06 compared with 1.94 for White youth. This means a young Black driver who gets stopped can expect to be stopped another 4 times in the next 12 months. Most stops did not result in any arrest, only five percent led to an offence being reported and only 3 percent to an arrest.[20]

Occasionally famous young Blacks make the media aware of this type of harassment. The Olympic athlete Linford Christie successfully sued the police for wrongful arrest when he was driving a hired car.[21] Barry Coy, a professional ice hockey player, was stopped more than 100 times in 1982 after buying a high performance rally car. He was never charged with any offence. The police could not cope with the idea that a young Black man could own an expensive car.[22]

The PSI study found the Metropolitan Police are less likely to stop men they classify as Asians mainly because their stereotyping of Asians is different, though no less racist. A common police view was that, 'Asians or Pakis are devious, sly or unreliable and in particular that they don't tell the truth.'[23]

The Immigration Act of 1971 gave impetus to racial harassment, and the police themselves extended its application well beyond the limits of the law. Schedule 2 of the 1971 Immigration Act authorised the arrest without warrant and the detention of suspected illegal immigrants by the police or Immigration Service. Those detained under this law have no right to bail and can be detained indefinitely. The Illegal Immigration Intelligence Unit of the police was set up by Scotland Yard without reference to Parliament in 1972.

The crudity of state racism in the Immigration and subsequent Nationality Acts is such that sections of the black population have been criminalised for what others would regard as responsible behaviour. It can be an offence to work (without a permit) and an offence not to work (failing to support dependants), or it may be illegal to attempt to unite or hold together an existing family.

The powers of arrest and detention are Kafkaesque, as when a deserted wife with her 14 year old daughter were held in Holloway prison awaiting deportation, because her husband had changed jobs seven years previously without official approval.[24]

The police have systematically refused to take racist attacks seriously. Two Parliamentary Home Affairs Committees have rebuked the police for failing to make racial assault a priority issue.

Figures have been produced on racial assaults which the Association of Chief Police Officers (ACPO), the Home Office and Scotland Yard all agree are gross underestimates. The police gave figures of what they termed 3,571 racial 'incidents' in 1985.[25] Other sources put the figure for racial attacks at 20,000 and pointed to more than 60 racist murders since 1970.[26] According to the 1983 Greater London Council Police Committee report:

> The police displayed a 'variety of non-responses', being reluctant to investigate, slow in getting on the scene, refusing to prosecute, giving misleading advice, and treating the victims of crimes as criminals themselves. In 1983, children had been shot at with airgun pellets; meat cleavers, Stanley knives and fire-bombs had figured in the arsenal of

racism; pensioners, students, shopkeepers and infants had been among the victims.[27]

In 1987 it was reported that one in four Black residents of Newham had been the victim of a racist attack, and that four out of five of those who reported the attacks to the police were dissatisfied with the handling of the case.[28]

When 8,000 Asians marched in Coventry in 1981 against a series of racially motivated attacks, the police response was to put 1,000 officers on duty and arrest 74 of the marchers.[29] Similarly, the police arrested the 'Bradford 12' for self defence measures and when there was a mobilisation against a fascist British National Party demonstration in 1989 the police moved in for a mass arrest of Asian youths and other anti racists in Dewsbury.

None of the government or police inspired studies give statistical details of the racial assaults made by the police themselves, including the deaths of Eusif Ryan, Stephen Boyle and Cynthia Jarrett in 1985; Anthony Lemard and Ahmar Qureshi in 1986 and Clinton McCurbin, Ahmed Katongole, Nenneh Jalloh and Anachu Anozie Osita in 1987.[30]

It is possible to gain a glimpse of the type of harassment and assault suffered by whole families at the hands of police by looking at some of the small percentage of civil actions against the police which are successful. These include over £50,000 paid to David and Lucile White for 'inhuman treatment' during a raid on their house; £130,000 paid to the wife of Winston Rose who died in police custody and another £12,500 paid to Winston's father after he was unlawfully arrested on a demonstration about his son; and Rupert Taylor who was awarded over £100,000 compensation after drug planting, assault, false imprisonment and malicious prosecution.[31]

Drug laws are extensively used against Blacks in Britain today just as in the colonial days liquor laws were used against the North American Indians and against the Irish.[32] The police have extensive powers under the Dangerous Drugs Act of 1971 and the Misuse of Drugs Act 1971.

Popular fears of hard drugs such as heroin have been used to justify attacks on Black people, even though the sellers and users of hard drugs are predominantly White. The over policing of Black social events such as the Notting Hill Carnival have all been justified on the grounds of 'searching for drugs' or arresting 'muggers'. In 1976 a massive policing operation caused mayhem for the first time at the Notting Hill Carnival. In 1987 the riot police moved onto the streets at dusk to end the carnival.

Black meeting places are continually raided. For example, in October 1974, 100 police with dogs and riot shields raided a Black youth club, The Carib, in Cricklewood. 12 youths were arrested, all were acquitted. In 1975 police raided the Four Acres West Indian club with dogs searching for a youth who had allegedly stolen a purse. Some Black meetings places have suffered police raids time and again. The Mangrove in London was invaded by police in May 1968, May 1970, May 1974, August 1976, August 1978 and June 1988.[33] Even family events are not free from police disruption. For example, when in June 1980 the police raided a christening party, four young men were subsequently acquitted of assault and obstruction.[34]

It might be thought that the police complaints system could be used to check the behaviour of the worst racist police attacks. Not so. The first investigative stage in the complaints procedure, even after its revision in 1984, lies in the hands of the police themselves. There is little protection or redress for Black victims within that procedure. Despite all the documentation of police racial assaults, between 1973 and 1978 no complaint of racial discrimination was upheld by the Metropolitan Police Complaints procedure.[35] In 1985 according to the Metropolitan Commissioners' Annual Report, 58 complaints of racial discrimination were reviewed. All were rejected.

The Police and Criminal Evidence Act 1984 included a provision to make racism a distinct disciplinary offence. This provision was strongly opposed by the Police Federation. By June 1986 no one had been disciplined.[36]

Periodically the police produce 'mugging' statistics to create fear of violent crime committed mostly by Black people. There is no indication, even on the most biased of the Metropolitan Police figures that more than 4 percent of West Indian youths commit crimes. But the racists at the top of the police hierarchy publicise and encourage the publication of racist crime statistics. This reinforces police racism at street level. If the spurious statistics are taken as hard fact by police constables, then this leads them to treat Black youths as automatic suspects, and make more Black arrests. So the vicious circle continues. As one police constable said, 'If so many... are involved in crime, why shouldn't we give them disproportionate attention'.[37] Stopping and searching can produce arrests for 'obstruction', 'breach of the peace' or 'assault' which add to the official record of Black 'crime'. The circle continues.

Resistance

PEOPLE HAVE fought back against the harassment which is legitimised under racist immigration laws and justified on the basis of searches for drugs and 'muggers'. In the early 1980s smouldering resentment, particularly among Black youth, blew up into riots. In the first instance in Bristol in April 1980, the police raided the Black and White Cafe, a meeting place for Black youth. This set off a fight back against the police, who were forced out of the area for a number of hours. In Brixton in April 1981 rioting broke out after police saturated the area with Special Patrol Group officers in an exercise called 'Operation Swamp' (echoing Margaret Thatcher's comment that: 'this country may be rather swamped by people of a different culture').[38] These reactions to police racism united Black and White in a struggle which brought many different resentments—over unemployment, bad housing, harassment—to a focus:

> the first Brixton riot broke when 'the police tried to arrest a Black guy... Black and White people went over to help'. The riot was a ... fair cross section of younger people, Black and White... in Bristol the crowd which drove back the police... was 'almost a third White'... In the case of Toxteth... some White youths seem to have been involved from the beginning and by the end of the night of rioting, the rioters were at least 50-50 Black and White. In Moss Side, of the 106 arrests... 78 were White ... In Halifax there was a 'right good mix of skinheads and Asian youth'...
> *In virtually all* the British riots there has been significant White involvement alongside Blacks, and the involvement has not just been of White leftists, but of White working class youth.[39]

The anti police riots in Britain in the 1980s were not on the scale of the ghetto risings in the US. Nevertheless, like the American uprisings, the British riots were sparked off by specific police actions. They were an angry reaction to police oppression, racism and social deprivation.

Although the police pick on those they classify as West Indian, White youths also come in for more police aggravation than do middle aged West Indians or Asians. Not only racism, but also harassment of working class youth in general lay behind the anti police rioting in Britain in the 1980s.[40] The fact that Asian youth were involved also shows both that they suffer at the hands of the police and are prepared to fight back.

The death of Cynthia Jarrett following a police raid and the shooting and paralysing by the police of Cherry Groce led to further anti police rioting in 1985. In Tottenham, there was a massive confrontation between police and people on the Broadwater Farm estate. Winston Silcott, Mark Braithwaite and Engin Raghip were all framed for murder after the death of PC Blakelock in the riot. The fit-up was finally admitted in 1991 when their sentences were quashed.

The riots highlighted a contradiction in policing. The police's role is to oppress and divide the working class. But attempts at oppression and division can become difficult once the oppression moves away from the bullying of individuals into violent collective confrontation. When the police move in heavily in the inner cities, black *and* white are affected. The violence of the operation reinforces police racism but can undermine working class racism as Black and White youth unite aginst a common enemy.

Aware of the unity that had been created, chiefs of police attempted in 1981 to redefine both White and Black street-fighters as criminals. Liverpool's Chief Constable Kenneth Oxford asserted:

> The trouble was caused by a criminal element who are hell bent on driving the police out of the area so that they could set up their little Mafia to commit crime without let or hindrance.[41]

The racism of the British police is not just a hangover from imperialism. Police racism is linked with the class role they perform and by the impossibility of the task set them of preventing crime. Examine in history the link between police, racism and class.

Three quarters of the cost of the early police came from propertied ratepayers who saw the police as their servants.[42] They felt themselves threatened by the poor.[43] Preventative policing was about 'watching and suspecting'. It was not possible to watch and suspect everyone who was poor. So the stereotyping of 'criminal types' was tied to the notion of preventative policing. As there is no such thing as a 'criminal type' this meant suspecting anyone who was easily recognisable. In the nineteenth century the stereotypes was the, 'stalwart Irish navvies ... wearing red handkerchiefs... at the corners of the street'.[44]

Stereotyping is still taught in police training. Officers are taught discredited racist psychology about physical types and criminal personality. In the police booklet **Catching Criminals, Some More Basic Skills**, the new constable is informed: 'the most important quality of a thief catcher is basically a question of being able to categorise or stereotype a person.' The good criminal catcher learns to differentiate 'between persons from different countries.[45] Constables are encouraged to look for clues to criminality such as dress, facial appearance, tattoos, voice, accent, hair, eyes and odour.[46] Who easier to recognise than the person with black skin?

The Rastafarian is to be treated according to one trainer, Chief Inspector Holland, as 'a criminal suspect'. Instead of the Irish stereotype of a century ago, the police target was to be 'the West Indian in tea cosy hats loitering in the city centres'. [47]

Police racism is not peculiar to Britain:

In the USA, academics measure changes in police/public relations in terms of the number of people shot dead annually by police officers, and the measure has particular significance because, in most cases, it is white police officers who kill black citizens.[48]

According to one study, Surinamers in Holland, 'provide the police with a reservoir of archetypal symbolic assailants— instantly visible and readily available'.[49] North Africans in France and Koreans in Japan suffer the same treatment.

As the crisis in world capitalism deepens it will become more important to the ruling class that workers adopt racist and nationalist ideas. As capitalist production becomes more integrated it becomes even more necessary to the bosses that workers in different parts of the world, wearing the same overalls and doing the same jobs should identify not with each other but with some spurious national interest. Racist police activity reinforces this notion of a uniform national identity.

Across the world, police racism is best understood by looking at the function performed by the police within capitalism rather than by looking at the composition of the police force or the characteristics of individual policemen. It certainly is not explicable in terms of the behaviour of those they police.

Chapter nine

Police, family and sex

SEXISM, LIKE racism, runs like a twisted thread through all police work. Prostitutes and gay men are harassed; lesbians treated with contempt. Cases of domestic violence are regarded as 'rubbish'. Rape victims are routinely thought to have been 'asking for it'. But, just as an overwhelmingly white force does not in itself explain police racism, the predominance of men does not explain why the police force is sexist.

Police activities in relation to sexual morality are best understood within the context of developing capitalism and the key role of the nuclear family. There is no historical tradition of the police protecting working class women from sexual violence. There is more evidence of police oppression and interference in the sexual morality of the working class.

In the nineteenth and early twentieth centuries the police harassed working class women and some men who expressed their sexuality outside the iron confines of the nuclear family. The 1851 census was the first to find that town dwellers outnumbered the rural population. Urbanisation was rapid. London's population grew from 2 to 5 million between 1841 to 1881, and Sheffield's from 111,000 to 285,000.[1] The urban upper and middle classes became afraid that their lives would be 'contaminated' by the influx of large numbers of working class men, women and children, often suffering from ill health or contagious diseases. These fears coincided with another concern: the spread of venereal diseases among the armed forces. The establishment aimed to control the women to whom the armed forces may have had access. In the mid nineteenth century laws were introduced which gave the police considerable powers over working class women and reflected, a new enthusiasm for state intervention in the lives of the poor on medical and sanitary grounds. The mid century sanitary movement created a close identification of public order and public health.[2]

A major attack on the sexuality of working class women involving police harassment, was launched under the Contagious Diseases Acts of the 1860s. A woman could be identified as a prostitute by special plain clothes policemen, and then subjected to a fortnightly internal examination. If found to be suffering from gonorrhoea or syphilis, she could be interned in a certified hospital for up to nine months. When accosted by the police, a woman had to submit voluntarily to medical and police registration, or else go before a local magistrate. If brought to trial for refusing to comply, the woman had responsibility for 'proving that she was virtuous, and that she did not go with men, whether for money or not'.[3] The repealers argued that the acts threatened 'modest' working women in the affected districts: 'There exists a fear [among] the respectable females to walk in the street after dark, lest they might be interfered with by the "spy police".'[4]

An alliance between middle class feminists and trade unionists campaigned to get rid of the acts.[5] Demonstrations were held and organised opposition led to their repeal in the 1880s. However, the acts had already led to the labelling of prostitutes as criminals.

The police have wide discretionary powers over prostitution which arise from the contradictory view of prostitution encouraged by our society. The activities of prostitutes undermine the idea of the one man, one woman married relationship, but also provide sexual relief for men outside marriage. Prostitution therefore threatens the ideology but preserves the institution of marriage. In the past the rich wanted sexual services, but feared the property claims of illegimate offspring. Legal paternity was difficult to establish by women branded as prostitutes.

Prostitutes were seen as a necessity for unsettled workers such as seamen, soldiers and casual labourers. But, as part of the street economy, prostitution lessened the pressure on women to enter disciplined wage labour. Prostitution allowed lower wages to be paid, as individual rather than collective solutions were sought by women to increase meagre earnings. Moreover, profits could be torn from prostitutes as they sold sex as a commodity.

In Britain, as in many other parts of the world, the police labelled and stigmatised the individual prostitute. But at the same time they allowed prostitution to continue. By shaming the prostitute, the ideology of the family was protected. Prostitutes were isolated both socially and geographically and thus the space of the middle and upper classes was protected. In Berlin in the 1830s prostitutes were licensed and regulated by the police, as they were in France in the same period. In Paris the rules stipulated that, 'brothels could not be within 100 yards of a church or 50 or 60 yards of a school, palace, public building or boarding house'.[6]

Police today regard prostitutes as 'criminals' although prostitution in Britain is not of itself a criminal offence. For example, at the time of the Yorkshire Ripper multiple murder case the police issued a statement in 1982, saying that, 'the Ripper, having previously murdered prostitutes, is now seeking victims amongst innocent women'.[7]

One particularly pernicious effect of the way in which the law deals with prostitution is that it makes it more difficult for prostitutes to protect themselves by working together. Brothels, defined as places where two or more prostitutes live, are outlawed.

Prostitutes have at times taken collective action. Following a series of murders of prostitutes and in protest against increasing police harassment, French prostitutes occupied a church in Lyons in 1975. The movement spread and led to collectives being set up in different parts of the world. Many feminists wrongly scorned the prostitutes, accusing them of degrading all women by allowing themselves to be sex objects.[8]

The prostitutes replied that the feminists were lining up with the police and instead of attacking the sex industry as a part of the capitalist system were instead 'attacking the workers in that industry.'[9]

They also rejected the idea that all prostitutes were part of a sisterhood, explaining that there was a wide difference in the earnings of the top 'call girls' and the street girls. The police treated the two types of prostitutes differently, leaving the call girls to get on with their business and arresting and imprisoning the street girls.

The prostitutes' collective pointed out they were fighting for women's rights:

> Prostitution is a matter of survival. Until government provides women with decent financial alternatives, no amount of police harassment and brutality can prevent us from feeding our families. No Vice Squad or Special Branch can stop mothers from loving and caring for their children and wanting a better life for them.[10]

The police have no scruples in breaking up the families of prostitutes because here the role of the family as the unit enforcing moral values is undermined. The banner across the Church at the time of the Lyons prostitutes' strike read: 'Our children don't want their mothers in jail'.[11]

Many people have seen the outlawing of prostitution as a solution to the way in which prostitutes alone are singled out for harassment. This, they argue will focus police powers against men who use prostitutes.

Patronising prostitutes became a violation of the criminal code in New York State in 1967. Police and businessmen opposed its introduction, but in the first month of the application of the new offence only 35 patrons were arrested and only one convicted. The average number of prostitutes arrested per month was 738.[12] When kerb crawling became an offence in Britain in 1985, some police forces issued letters to identified crawlers but didn't arrest them. In March 1988, 134 prostitutes were arrested in Balsall Heath in Birmingham, but only 29 kerb crawlers.[13]

Campaigns seeking equality of repression can increase police powers and divert attention away from the root causes of the problem. The kerb crawling law increased the dangers for prostitutes by giving them less time to assess the risk of violence from potential clients.[14] History gives us examples of the dangers in seeking equality of sexual oppression.

Victorian working class families feared low wages or unemployment would force women into prostitution. But the anger and fear were diverted from the economic roots of the problem.

Crusades against the 'White Slave Trade' and child prostitution focused on foreign slavers seeking girls for brothels abroad rather than on low wages at home. Feminists who had rightly campaigned with trade unionists against the Contagious

Diseases Acts turned towards equality of sexual oppression for men. This idea crystallised in the slogan 'Votes for women and chastity for men!'[15] Massive rallies were held to raise the age of consent. The laws which resulted from the campaign did little to lessen abuse but gave the police even more powers to intervene in working class lives on allegedly moral grounds. The Criminal Law Amendment Acts of 1885 and 1912 did little to protect anyone. The socialist Sylvia Pankhurst remarked of the 1912 act: 'It is a strange thing that the... Act which was passed ostensibly to protect women is used almost exclusively to punish women'.[16] The 1885 act, which raised the age of consent from 13 to 16, was used frequently against working class youth and rarely against the rich. The same act contained a section making homosexuality between consenting males illegal.

Sexual relationships for men outside the nuclear family were criminalised. The family, by the late nineteenth century, had become the essential unit for reproducing, maturing and controlling the growing labour force. The family became an, 'area of private sex life, separated from the public sphere of production, but one ordered and controlled by capitalism'.[17]

The police played an important role in curbing the sexual freedom which might otherwise have become a possibility for those escaping religious-dominated rural communities.

Police harassment of gay men and lesbians and the law's long refusal to recognise them as suitable for forming families to bring up children was part of capitalism's aggressive attempt to make the nuclear family the only approved living arrangement. The law also attempted to ensure that the sexual divisions implied by the family were passed on to future generations of workers. `

Victorian morality stretched its dirty tentacles well into the twentieth century. The extent of police harassment of gays has been partly determined by the degree of bigotry of chief constables in particular areas. For example, the year before the appointment of James Anderton as Chief Constable of Manchester there had been two prosecutions for male importuning. After his appointment, prosecutions ran at an average of 118 a year.[18]

The Gay Liberation Movement started in America to fight police oppression and end the commercial exploitation of gay men. On 17 June 1969, some two hundred gays were crowded into the Stonewall bar in New York. Like many other gay bars, the mafia ran it, paying off the police, who made occasional raids without hitting the bar owners. On that night the crowd fought off a police raid and three days of fighting followed. The police were beaten. In August the Gay Liberation Front was set up. In Britain the struggle for gay liberation was carried on a rising tide of working class confidence. Homosexuality between consenting male adults had been made legal in 1967. Although gays and lesbians had some legal rights, police continued to trap gays for 'cottaging'. Lesbians had to fight court battles to retain custody of their children. Gay pride was a hard fight and made little impact on the muck of ages coagulating in police ideology. As late as 1981 the Police Federation issued the following statement:

> While the Police Federation accepts that homosexual conduct between consenting males over the age of 21 ought not to be a criminal offence, it deplores the way official thinking on this subject appears to be surrendering to the pressure groups, who try to persuade society that homosexual conduct is perfectly normal.[19]

Gays are still arrested because of the high age of consent (21 years). Home Office research has shown that of those people convicted of homosexual offences in England and Wales, the vast majority had been involved in consenting behaviour. The spread of HIV has led to further scapegoating of gays. For example, one particularly obscene police raid was reported in 1987:

> Police wearing rubber gloves raided the Vauxhall Tavern, a gay London pub early on Saturday and arrested eleven persons for drunkenness.[20]

Section 28 of the Local Government Act of 1988 reiterated the obsession with the nuclear family, making illegal the teaching of the 'acceptability of homosexuality as a pretended family relation'. In 1991 the attack continued with Clause 25 of the Criminal Justice Bill intended to put homosexual behaviour on the same level as child abuse and indecent assault. Convictions for 'indecency'—showing affection in public—increased by 106 percent between 1985 and 1989. Guidelines were also issued by the Tory government to stop lesbians and gays from fostering children.[21]

Women in the force

THE WOMEN'S police force originated in the disintegration of the suffragette movement in the First World War. Some suffragettes were appalled by the treatment of women victims in court. They themselves had been the subject of considerable police brutality. But when they eventually entered the police force they became instrumental, not in protecting the rights of working class women, but in repressing and controlling them.

The ruling class feared the spread of sexually transmitted diseases among the troops, and the womens' patrols were used to keep soldiers and working class women apart. At its crudest in the town of Grantham, where there was a military establishment of 25,000 and a civilian population of 20,000, women were under curfew between 7pm and 8am.

The suffragette movement split as to whether they should involve themselves in operating the curfew! A group of them agreed to help enforce it. They began, 'seeking out immorality' among women with husbands at the front.[22] They broke up courting couples, as well as helping to police women munitions workers and prevent strikes.[23]

There seems to have been little questioning of the right of the upper classes to interfere in the sex lives of working class women. There was a crude assumption of superior morality. A question was raised about the social class of the early policewomen in a parliamentary committee. Lord Colesby queried:

> With regard to the class of women you employ. You obviously want an intelligent class of woman... but how far down the social scale do you actually go?

The reply was given:

> We have a number of bus conductresses. I hardly know to what class they belong. Those I should think are about the limit.[24]

It is clear from the history of the early women's park patrols in London that they protected the parks rather than women. They were concerned with women's 'decency' and children's behaviour—control, not protection.

In the 1950s one writer suggested having police dogs on the

Table 8. Women patrols, returns of work, 1919 (2 June-30 November) and 1921[25]

Cautions for:	1919	1921
Violation of public decency	3,952	4,856
Soliciting	1,030	3,362
Loitering	152	24,140
Men annoying females	40	-
Persons begging	184	1,617
Damaging property	1,964	7,575
Lighting fires	30	-
Trespassing	308	-
Riotous behaviour	1,695	4,929
Breach of Hyde Park Regulations:		
1. Bathing regs.	24	-
2. Cycling, football etc.	-	7,409
Using obscene language	5	4,209
Children riding behind vehicles	49	12,031

loose in public parks at night.[26] Ostensibly, these would root out sexual harassers, but presumably they wouldn't be able to distinguish these from lovers.

Victorian morality and police activity in moral policing diminished with changes which occurred in Britain after the Second World War. Medical breakthroughs made sexually transmitted diseases less of a threat, improved contraception meant that the link between sex and reproduction was less rigid and blood testing meant that paternity could be proved without women's fidelity.

The economic boom, particularly in the 1960s, introduced a new era of more enlightened sexual attitudes. The women's movement and the gay liberation movement of the early 1970s also helped to undermine the iron clad Victorian morality. The police were less obtrusive and family control slightly less rigid. This did not, however, get rid of sexism. According to a Policy Studies Institute report:

> The dominant values of the Force are still in many ways those of all male institutions such as the rugby club or boys'

school... the stress on drinking as a test of manhood... the importance given to physical courage and the glamour attached to violence. This set of attitudes and norms amount to a 'cult of masculinity' which also has strong influence on policemen's behaviour towards women, towards victims of sexual offences and towards sexual offenders.[27]

These attitudes underpin police treatment of victims of rape. A horrific example of the difficulty experienced by women in putting a rape charge was shown by the case of Jacqueline Berkeley, a young black woman. She was convicted of 'wasting police time' and given a suspended sentence of two years because she was courageous enough to complain of rape by two police officers at Moss Side police station in Manchester.[28] In a TV documentary on the Thames Valley police a rape victim was heavily interrogated by police officers.[29] The police did not argue for the interview to be edited out of the programme, indicating that it was seen as normal police practice.

Cross examining rape victims on the assumption that they were lying was a recommended practice in Britain and the US in the 1970s. For example, the Chicago police training manual instructed officers that, 'the first thing to do is to determine if the woman who reports the rape is lying'.[30] An extract from 'Rape, Police and Forensic Procedure' in the **Police Review** said of a woman complaining of rape:

> Allow her to make a statement to a police woman, and then drive a horse and cart through it. It is always advisable if there is any doubt about the truthfulness of her allegations to call her an outright liar.[31]

The TV interview mentioned above led to protests and demonstrations about the treatment of rape victims. As a result there was a change in official police attitudes. A pastel coloured training room and special course was set up at the Hendon Police College and some forces opened special rape units. But the improvements, whilst welcome, were not dramatic. It should be remembered that Jacqueline Berkeley's conviction for wasting police time occurred *after* these publicised reforms were supposed to have been made. The fact is police treatment of rape victims arises from police sexism too deep rooted to be cured by cosmetic treatment.

Can increasing police numbers or powers reduce the incidence of rape? It has taken 250 years to establish that rape in marriage constitutes a criminal offence, such is the extent to which the oppression of women through the family is embedded in our society.

The first national survey on rape within marriage showed that women were seven times more likely to be raped by their husband than by a stranger.[32] It is precisely because most rapes occur in the home either of the victim or the rapist that the police cannot be effective in preventing it. Increasing police powers will not protect women by cutting down the incidence of rape. In the United States when there was a death penalty for rape it did not lower the incidence.

Changing criminal law and police powers alone cannot reduce the distortions in sexuality expressed in rape, that are related to capitalist reduction of people to commodities with 'ideal' gender roles: obscene Rambo-type Action Men and silly Barbie Doll women.

There is no point in pressing for increased police power to control pornography. In Britain anti porn legislation has been used against political publications such as **The Little Red School Book** and against gay bookshops. State suppression of porn simply raises its price and fills the pockets of police vice squads as they issue unofficial licences to big business in the trade.[33]

Anti pornography campaigns quickly move into alliances with extreme right wing fanatics. The following extract explains this point well:

> By divorcing the issue of pornography from any real connection to the oppression of women, the Women Against Porn campaign guarantees that it will result in no challenge at all to the degradation of women in society. Any serious challenge to the 'violations of women's rights' has to target the system which is reponsible, not ally itself with those who are organising to defend the system.[34]

And on the broader questions of male violence and sexist ideas:

> individual workers do and say sexist things, or dominate their wives or even inflict violence upon women. This is one of the horrible ironies of the capitalist system. As long as

most people accept ruling class ideas and the working class remains divided, capitalists don't need to rely on massive repression to enforce their rule—individual people actually carry out the terror and the violence that the system produces.[35]

The police cannot prevent rape or violence within the home. The incidence of these crimes in time and space prevent this possibility in most cases. Ideas can change however when the whole baggage of ruling class ideology is questioned. Rape is not some fixed aspect of human behaviour. There have been societies where rape was virtually unkown. For example AT Bryant, writing about the Zulus between 1883 and 1935, reported only one single case of rape during that time.[36]

Attacking sexual oppression means attacking the class system which gives rise to the ideology and which the police help to sustain. Nowhere is this clearer than in respect of police attitudes generally towards violence within the family.

Recruiting women into the police force did not change police attitudes about the sanctity of the family. The first police women quickly adapted to police practices. As Joan Locke says, one of the rules the early police women were taught was to,

> never interfere in husband and wife disputes... the theory being that she would always change her mind and probably turn against you... besides... she quite enjoyed it really.[37]

The police do not operate to protect the interests of women and children or protect individuals from sexual harassment. They arrive, often reluctantly, if at all, after the event. Real social horrors do exist. But the police are in no position, and have no will, to do anything real about the problems.

The idea that the police have a loving concern for children is also a nonsense. The preservation of the nuclear family in the latter half of the nineteenth century took precedence over any concern for the children within the family. Lord Shaftesbury, flaunted as a fighter against child labour, was opposed to state intervention to stop cruelty in the family. The Royal Society for the Prevention of Cruelty to Animals predated the National Society for the Prevention of Cruelty to Children by 50 years, and some of the early child protection cases were fought on the basis that children were animals and therefore had the right to some protection from the state. It was not until 1889 in Britain that cruelty by parents became a criminal offence.

In the mid 1980s child abuse began to be taken seriously in Britain. Under the umbrella term was included not just physical cruelty and sexual abuse but also neglect arising from poverty. It was located in the family, not as a social problem, but as an individual problem to be solved by punishment. 'Bad parents' were criminalised and 'incompetent' social workers scapegoated. Children were whipped away and temporarily institutionalised or put in 'proper' families to minimise risk. Places of Safety orders proliferated without any increase in child care facilities or resources.

Professional carers became the villains, particularly in the Cleveland case in 1987, when a large number of children were removed from their parents on the slenderest of medical evidence. In all this the police were presented as uniformed protectors of children. The problems of the pressures within the nuclear family, unemployment, bad housing, lack of child care, low incomes and the distortion of sexuality were forgotten. Police powers were increased further under the 1989 Children Act, which may well be used to harass homeless teenagers.

If the idea is rejected that state forces can somehow be persuaded or trained to do something about the problem of male violence, do we have to sit back and 'wait for the revolution'? No, we should struggle, with the emphasis on collective action to wrest reforms and protection from the system rather than against individual men.

Any gain which takes some of the pressure out of families by giving men or women more freedom to get out of impossible family situations helps to protect women and children. These include decent wages, access to good housing, day nurseries and child care facilities, jobs and good social security provision. The funding of rape crisis centres or women's aid refuges are all important demands that can be made. Struggles for proper mental health care, and against hospital closures which force people back into community care where communities do not exist are also vital.

But the increase in police powers and the setting up of specially trained police units does nothing to prevent violence in the family either against women or against children. Social problems cannot be solved by the exercise of state force and increased use of prison. There is no simple penal solution to problems whose roots lie deep within the nature of society.

Chapter ten

Sport and the Kop

SPORTS AND pastimes are social activities which can either bring workers together, or can be used to set them against each other. Historically the authorities have responded to this contradiction with a high level of police intervention in order to try and achieve the most favourable outcome.

The aim, according to one historian, was to, 'promote the moral improvement of the labouring classes by the exercise of supervision and restraint'.[1] The link between control over leisure and political activities was plainest in the case of pubs. Patrick Colquhoun, an early advocate of the police,

> enumerated fifteen forms of misconduct, any one of which should be sufficient to cause a landlord to lose his licence. These included permitting combinations of workmen, meetings of societies or political clubs for 'seditious or traitorous designs'; holding out allurements by 'idle and sedentary' games; allowing 'idle amusements' such as boxing and cock fighting.[2]

The Bow Street Runners, precursors of the police, were required to 'disperse an illegal music meeting'.[3] John Fielding one of the 'pioneers of police reform' urged that 'ballad singers should be considered as vagabonds, liable to the same punishment'.[4] On the other hand there was a view that ballad singers,

> Might be rendered instruments useful under the control of a well regulated Police, in giving a better turn to the minds of the lower classes of people... According to his plan the police should be entrusted with the propagation of moral influences by issuing and distributing to the ballad singers

literature by which they could convey in language familiar to the working class moral lessons on advantages of industry and frugality, happiness of a good husband, good father and honest man and pleasure of absenteeism from public houses.[5]

The aim was to police the poor in order to increase productive labour. There were different standards for the rich. Gambling and drinking were deemed 'demoralising' for the poor and virtuous for the rich. One of the Fielding brothers, who established the Bow Street Runners in 1750, said:

To the upper part of mankind, time is the enemy and ... their chief labour is to kill it. Whereas with the other, time and money are almost synonymous, and they have little of each to spare, it becomes the legislature as much as possible to suppress all temptations whereby they may be induced too profusely to squander either the one or the other, since all such profusion must be repaired at the cost of the public. Such places of pleasures, therefore, as are totally set apart for the use of the great world, I meddle not with.[6]

In other words, if leisure activities could be confined to the good and the great, society would not be much affected. Henry Fielding, half-brother to John Fielding, expressed the same idea of removing from working men 'all Temptations to Idleness'.[7] The new police forces led to an,

entirely uncustomary surveillance of the entire range of popular leisure activity, drinking, brutal sports, foot racing, fairs, feasts and other fetes. The police came as unwelcome spectators into the very nexus of urban neighbourhood life.[8]

Yet the police themselves have never lived up to the moral standards they are charged with imposing on others. Between 1831 and 1837 the police made over 179,000 arrests for drunkenness.[9] However, a huge number in their own ranks had to be dismissed for drink-related lapses:

Of 214 constables appointed to form the new Cheshire Constabulary in 1850 ... 112 had been discharged within three years, 65 of them in the first twelve months. By far the most frequent cause of dismissal in all forces was drunkenness.[10]

More recently, the authors of the 1983 PSI report discovered that many CID 'working days',

> include a substantial period in the pub; and while drinking in pubs, CID officers are often 'on duty' or 'working overtime'... Also CID officers at all ranks often drink in the office; in many CID offices there is a regular drinking session, often on a Friday... CID officers are expected and required to drink.[11]

Sporting discipline

THE RISE OF sports under capitalism revealed double standards between what was expected of the rich and the poor. Nowhere was this clearer than with the case of 'blood sports'.

The earliest form of entertainment laid on by the state was the human blood sport of public executions. They were staged as carnival events and drew enormous multitudes of people. They were dramatic performances with huge, excited audiences with class terror at the centre of the stage and stewarded by soldiers pointing rifles at the crowds. Once the working class started showing its muscle in the nineteenth century these bloody entertainments declined.

Working class sports involving animal rather than human blood were regarded as brutal by the ruling class. Moreover, they sometimes interfered with work. In the mid nineteenth century the police clamped down on working class sports which drew big crowds. Bear baiting, cock and dog fighting were made illegal. According to one account:

> Between January and July near Bradford a state of open warfare existed between local inhabitants and the new police... at the end of January there was a crackdown on cockfighting and a number of men were arrested and fined 5/- for cruelty to animals.[12]

Harsh punishment was given to peasants who poached animals for food, who ate the game which was to be preserved for the rich to kill just for pleasure. In Scotland sheep farmers were cleared from the Highlands to make way for deer forests and grouse moors. The case of the huntsman prosecuted in 1985 for cockfighting shows such stark hypocrisy lives on.[13]

Any street sport taken up by working class youth in the nineteenth and early twentieth century was the object of police attention. The co-operation of the police today for commercially sponsored road marathons and fun runs contrasts very much with the attitude to working class road runners in Britain in the nineteenth century. For example it is recorded that,

> By the end of December 1856... the roads of Wakefield [were being] habitually 'infested with young men given to foot racing', [and these] were being cleared by the new police.[14]

Swimming was a popular pastime among working class children and adolescents. They didn't have shorts, so they swam in the nude, thereby breaking local bylaws, 'and provoked an angry response from the police and park attendants'.[15] An often used early photograph shows an irate police woman with a stick chasing nude youngsters along the banks of the Serpentine in the 1920s.

Just as today the police continually stop and question young motorcyclists, so in the 1890s cyclists were a 'menace to society'. The bicycling craze of the 1890s led to a social panic:

> It was feared that the push bike was a health hazard, for example causing 'bicycle face' and 'bicycle foot' as well as the dreaded *kyphosis bicyclistratum*, or 'cyclist hump' which resulted if the handlebars were set too low. Evidence placed before the Physical Deterioration Committee even suggested that cycling was a threat to the nation's manliness inducing varicocele of the testicles, 'from the pressure of the saddle'.[16]

Media headlines screamed of 'The Cyclist Terror', the 'Perils of the Wheel', 'The Dangers of City Cycling' and 'Cyclomania'.[17] There were many complaints by cyclists of harassment by the police.

When a cyclist was found not guilty of a hit and run offence the press suggested that, 'There were cyclists on the jury, we read, and this fact has a grim sound... Steps should be taken to put these people down'.[18]

Even ramblers met with police interference as youngsters were organised to get out of the cities into the surrounding countryside. This conflict became most intense during the 1930s depression. Five youths were imprisoned after a mass trespass by over 500 across the grouse shooting moors to Kinder Scout in 1932.[19]

Of all the sports in Britain, football has probably the longest tradition as a workers' sport and the most continuous history of police intervention. Breaking up games of street football went on from the 1890s to the 1930s. And, although regulations were considered 'necessary precaution for the protection of life and property and the smooth flow of traffic', the police were often 'petty and brutal in their treatment of those who resisted the laws and continued to play street football'.[20]

Stopping street games seems to have been an important police activity during the 1920s. In Islington, for example, over half the reported arrests of juveniles were connected with either football or pitch and toss.[21] Even in the 1980s the police summonses and charges handbook noted it was an offence to,

> play football (or other game (specify)) on a certain highway (specify) to the annoyance of (name) a user thereof, contrary to section 140 (3) Highways Act 1959.[22]

The criminalisation of street activities often provoked fierce resistance. But the question of sport and the working class eventually met with a change in upper class attitudes. Recruitment during the Boer War revealed how many working class youths were not fit enough to fight and stimulated a new concern for their health and physical fitness. Some of the ruling class wondered if the force and energy shown in street sport could not be channelled into some useful activity like dying for the Empire. There was also the possibility that, 'if you provide them with footballs they would not be so inclined to kick the police.'[23]

There was a move to channel and discipline the energy of working class youth into organised sport, which was seen as 'disciplining and character building'. The development of Boys Clubs, the Boy Scouts and Boys' Brigade with their emphasis on sport, physical fitness and Empire was going on at the same time as the police were clearing the streets of the spontaneous and self organised sporting activities of the working class.

Spectator sport became a source of profit and football in particular became big business. But the sheer numbers and collective excitement of the game caused the ruling class some anxieties. Baden Powell spoke of football crowds groaning and cheering in 'panic unison'.[24] There are many press references to football supporters as vulgar and noisy, and when the Football League was set up in 1880, its supporters from the industrial heartlands of northern England were referred to as 'hooting, yelling mobs'.[25]

Ruling class fear of workers shouting in mass chorus was echoed by David Phillips, then Assistant Chief Constable of Greater Manchester, at a 1987 International Conference on soccer violence when he said,

> individual shouts and gestures mean nothing but 20,000 chanting in unison... create an emotionally charged atmosphere... It is all about whether or not behaviour can create that sense of power and energy.[26]

Football hooliganism is often presented as a worrying new development. But,

> there is a well documented history of pitch invasions, attacks on referees and players, and fighting between rival fans throughout the latter part of the nineteenth century and into the new century... In 1893, spectators burst onto the field during a game between Nottingham Forest and West Bromwich Albion, and a fight ensued between players and fans... in 1888, another referee complained bitterly about his ill treatment by a Bolton crowd ... In the same year a Northern sporting rag reported how 'a continuous hail of empty bottles' had showered the pitch.[27]

One of the problems in looking at violence amongst football crowds is that it is in the interests of the ruling class to exaggerate its seriousness. It is therefore difficult to extract the facts. What is very clear however is that the most violent and hideous tragedies have more to do with unsafe grounds and overcrowding than with fights between rival fans. Profit has a greater savagery than the wildest of fans.

In the 1980s alone 412 deaths were recorded at football matches directly caused by crushes or structural collapse. Indeed, some of the tragedies were sparked off by police firing shots and causing panic, leading to fatal crushes in Lima in 1964, Tripoli in 1968, Port au Prince in 1976 and Brazil in 1982.

In 1985 there was the horror of the fire in the Bradford stadium killing 56, and the deaths when the wall collapsed at the

Table 9. The toll of soccer business violence[28]

Year	Place	Dead	Injured	Circumstances
1902	Ibrox, Glasgow	26	500	stand collapsed
1914	Hillsborough, Sheffield	-	75	wall collapsed
1946	Bolton	33	400	wall collapsed
1961	Santiago, Chile	5	35	?
1961	Ibrox	3	35	stand collapsed
1964	Lima, Peru	318	500	police fired-panic
1968	Argentina	74	150	stadium fire
1968	Tripoli	30	120	police fired-panic
1971	Ibrox	69	100	stairway crush
1972	Wolverhampton	-	80	barrier collapsed
1974	Turkey	44	600	platform collapsed
1975	Moscow	20	?	light failed-panic
1976	Haiti	6	?	police fired-panic
1978	Orient, London	-	30	barrier collapsed
1979	Cairo	48	-	wall collapsed
1979	Indonesia	12	?	panic and crush
1981	Middlesborough	2	-	pillar collapsed
1981	Columbia	17	15	stand collapsed
1981	Greece	21	54	stairway crush
1982	Colombia	24	50	crowd crush
1982	Algiers	8	600	stand collapsed
1982	Moscow	69	?	barrier broke
1982	Brazil	3	25	police fired-panic
1985	Birmingham	1	20	wall collapsed
1985	Mexico	10	74	crowd crush
1985	Heysel, Belgium	39	250	wall collapsed
1985	Holland	50	?	?
1985	Bradford	56	200	stand fire
1988	Katmandu	71	200	locked gate-crush
1989	Hillsborough	95	170	crowd crush

Heysel stadium in Belgium killing 39.[29] Fighting led to the crush, but it was structural failure that caused the deaths at Heysel. The Bradford fire was, almost certainly started by a lighted cigarette dropped accidentally through a gap underneath the seating where debris had collected for at least seventeen years.[30]

Yet at the time, the Bradford fire was not explained in terms of penny pinching by football bosses but linked instead to 'disorder and hooliganism' which had nothing whatsoever to do with the fire. The Popplewell Report on the Bradford fire was extended away from safety to look at 'control' in football stadiums.

Policing is now very heavy in British stadiums. According to that same report, in 1979 there was on average one policeman to every 1,000 spectators at league matches. In 1985 the average was nearer one in 75.[31]

The worst ever football disaster in Britain showed intensive policing did not enhance safety. The tragedy at the Hillsborough ground in Sheffield during the Liverpool-Nottingham Forest cup semi final on 15 April 1989—when 95 people were killed and hundreds injured—raised in macabre horror the real function of police at football matches.

For a start, they created the situation which led to disaster. The police opened the gate at the Lepping Lane end of the stadium, allowing thousands to pour into a packed centre stand out of which people were trying to escape. The police insisted on the installation of the perimeter fences behind which fans were trapped and crushed as a precondition for their not opposing a safety certificate. The police failed to convey to the club a report they had received from the fire service that the method of recording the numbers of fans was dangerous because it did not indicate the numbers in each pen.[32] The police had enormous resources. It had been their boast that:

> The video cameras now at our disposal are highly sophisticated. They can supervise the movement of supporters inside and outside the ground ... there will be no escape from the all seeing eye of the police.[33]

Surveillance, intelligence gathering, sophisticated equipment and the 770 officers at Hillsborough had nothing to do with crowd safety and everything to do with control.

The Hillsborough tragedy made clear that crowd control was in conflict with crowd safety. Both the Hillsborough and Bradford tragedies showed that the police had not been trained in crowd evacuation and they had no more knowledge about first aid than the fans. In 1985 Manchester Chief Constable James Anderton gave an interview to the football magazine **Shoot** in which he said:

> We want better segregation and an improvement in physical barriers at grounds. People will go where they are put.[34]

It is part of police duty to keep people penned in, dangerous though the practice is. No one has ever been killed in a pitch invasion. But cutting off that escape route has cost lives. The Green Code on Ground Safety published after a disaster at Ibrox in 1971 stated clearly, 'the best place to evacuate everyone is the pitch'. But the tiny perimeter gate at Hillsborough was only wide enough to let police or ambulance workers to enter. It was useless for mass evacuation.[35]

Underneath this penning of fans is that fear of predominantly working class crowds that runs through any history of policing and spectator sport. The contempt for football supporters was expressed at the time of Hillsborough by Jacques Georges, President of UEFA, European football's governing body, in a TV interview. He said that he had gained the impression that the fans outside the ground were, 'beasts who wanted to charge into the arena. It was not far short of hooliganism'.[36] Precisely the same sort of filth is contained in a public statement by one high ranking police officer who said, 'Some were like animals drunk and violent. Their actions were vile.'[37]

Yet while the police's obsession with social control led to the massacre of fans at Hillsborough, it was the fans themselves who organised the efforts to rescue the stricken supporters.

The carpet of flowers and endless silent queues at the Liverpool and Sheffield grounds after the tragedy said something different to police accounts. Such was the respect shown to the victims and heroes of Hillsborough that even the right wing **Daily Express** was forced into printing an uncharacteristic outburst:

> the game is awash with cash—from lotteries, pools, TV contracts and the like. Unfortunately it's not being spent on the people who pay out most of it—the poor bloody infantry who every Saturday are searched, segregated and frog-

marched in police lines onto some concrete wasteland to peer through steel mesh.[38]

The **Sun** newspaper lost 250,000 readers after Hillsborough for publishing lies about the fans.[39]

Out of Hillsborough came horror and anger at the police and the Football Association but also something else. Here is the account from Liverpool fan Robert Kincaid who describes both the horror and the heroism of Hillsborough as he saw it from one of the terraces:

> This wasn't the telly, it was happening down there. There was a line of policemen and people looking around desperately for their friends and shouting names. There's anger at the photographers: 'fucking parasites'. Then the comments from behind, 'Look down there. Look at the guy in the yellow, they're pumping his chest. They've covered him up.' I was stood there in tears. 'He's gone him... he's bloody gone'. There was a sheet over him—same thing over there... They were big hefty blokes, they could have had a heart attack and then I saw a kid of about twelve covered up, that's when I began to realise... They were being carried off. I was sick. I refused to accept they were dead. They weren't being crushed any more, they were just lying in the sun. Their limbs were all there, the way they had been made, Why couldn't somebody just snap their fingers and make them live again. A guy near us tried to kill himself and we had to hold him back... Still we'd only seen one ambulance... The people were brilliant. It was disgusting, the abuse of fans in the papers. The people were brilliant. The people were helping all the way. There were more people helping than the police, the police never had the initiative to tear down the advertising boards and use them as stretchers. The police weren't the ones who started ripping down the cages. It was the fans. They did everything. They were the ones who knew what was happening. Everyone knew the match had to be abandoned. They wouldn't have wanted it otherwise, but when the announcement was made: 'keep your tickets for the replay'. The crowd roared its disgusted anger'.[40]

There was a community that was inspiring at Hillsborough but it wasn't that of the police or the football bosses. Those police standing as a divisive force in the centre of the pitch weren't a part of it and like the bosses didn't understand it or have the capacity for organisation as the fans themselves took control.

The distorted myths of football hooliganism have been used more widely to help gain public acceptance for public order legislation and increased surveillance and crowd control technology. One of the recommendations of the Popplewell Report after the Bradford fire was for the introduction of identity cards; a ludicrous irrelevance to the disaster and rightly seen as a dangerous policy because of the creation of impatient crushes outside grounds, an argument reinforced by the Hillsborough tragedy. Nevertheless, the government tried to push ahead with the scheme.

Major sporting events involving large numbers can be used as police training exercises for overtly political events. For example it is not particularly unusual to see police helicopters overhead at major political demonstrations. The Metropolitan Police Commission Report for 1956 had this to say of their use:

> The possible uses of helicopters for police duty continues to be explored and experiments were conducted at Wembley on the day of the FA Cup Final and at Epsom on Derby day. These afforded interesting experience in the control of crowds and traffic from the air, and also enabled the Civil Defence officials, who participated to study the movement of large numbers of people and vehicles to and from confined spaces and over wide areas.[41]

Even here, in a corner of social activity seemingly far removed from politics, we find the search for profits and social order weighing down on the backs of the working class. Here too, therefore, we also find the police.

Chapter eleven

Crime: the problem redefined

THE LAW AND order lobby miss the most fundamental points about their specialist subject—the roots and causes of crime.

The narrow definition of crime in our society precludes most of the greatest horrors visited on humans by other humans and thereby absolves the rich and the powerful. Children are killed and maimed in wars or die of malnutrition when food is plentiful, yet this doesn't officially count as child abuse. Old people die of hypothermia, but that doesn't count as violence.

Crime as it is defined in our society is overwhelmingly to do with two things. The first is interpersonal violence. It is much more concerned, however, about property rights—the right of those with property to keep it out of the hands of those without. This covers the personal and corporate wealth of the rich, but also extends to concerns about public order in general as breakdowns in public order can threaten the ability of the establishment to control the wealth of society as a whole.

There's no doubt crime can blight the lives of ordinary people. Most crimes are committed by working class people against other working class people. By and large rich youths don't break into working class homes to steal money or stereos—they don't need to. And, sadly, most of the minority of working class youths who do commit such offences end up taking the meagre possessions of other people who live on the same estates and have little themselves.

Moreover, the same economic pressures which drive people to property crime also have a—less direct—effect on the incidence of interpersonal violence and its impact on people's lives.

The official statistics exaggerate the proportion of crime committed by the working class, as the working class are policed more harshly, have less privacy, less institutional protection than the middle classes and are more likely to be prosecuted, found guilty and jailed.[1] However, even though middle and upper class interpersonal and property crime may go unreported, the pressure on the wealthy to commit offences is considerably less than on those living in poor conditions with low incomes.

A Home Office study in 1990 stressed that, 'economic factors have a major influence on trends in both property and personal crime.'[2] The research supports the simple but subversive idea that people are more likely to steal when they cannot afford to buy:

> Throughout the post war period consumption growth has almost exactly mirrored the growth of property crime... The relationship is so strong that the last two decades of British economic history are in effect written into the history of recorded crime during the same period, with each peak and trough in the economy being accurately mirrored by a trough and a peak in the growth of crime undertaken for gain.[3]

The study also found a, 'Growth in offences of violence against the person... to be associated with growth in unemployment, and the relation is strong.'[4]

Capitalism creates gross inequalities of income and makes commodities more important than people. Greed, ambition and competitiveness are business virtues. Women are used as sex objects to sell products. Material possessions and high status jobs are measures of success denied to the majority of workers. The system creates meaningless labour so that living has to be packed into the few hours that workers can call their own. It takes away identity from the unemployed and leaves empty days. It puts impossible strains on the family.

Working class women are more likely to be raped, working class families are more likely to be victims of theft, assault, burglary or vandalism than well heeled residents elsewhere. The working class are more likely to be both victims and offenders in relation to crimes of property and violence. Many of these crimes have a serious impact on people's lives. Domestic violence, neglected by the police, is devastating. Even small thefts from people on tiny incomes can have a serious impact.

These most fundamental causes of crime—poverty and

alienation—are systematically ignored by the police and the rest of the establishment as they seek to blame crime on bad parents, subversive teachers or low moral standards.

Yet reducing inequality and ensuring that those out of work had a proper income would be the most obvious way of cutting crime. The tension and stress created by poverty increase and bring in their turn more violence and sexual offences. The roots of crime lie in the nature of the economic system and the type of society it spawns.

This is not to argue that *all* crime is economically determined. Many people live in poverty and do not steal. Not all sexually frustrated people become sex offenders and stress does not necessarily produce a violent response. All bored youths don't smash up bus shelters or fire pellets through old people's windows. Individuals very often have choices. But the alternatives may be severely limited. A homeless person may choose to sleep under a bridge or in a doorway, a warm bed is not on offer. The violent offender often feels cornered and sees no escape other than through violence.

Whereas choices are closed down at the bottom of society, they are opened up at the top. The wealthy don't have to choose between food or heat. Rich youths don't have to steal fast cars for kicks, they have their own. Upper class women can afford to escape from a violent relationship into an alternative home. High income increases choices. Poverty creates individual powerlessness, reduces choice and creates tensions so that a criminal option can seem the only way out.

All of this could be common sense, but in the topsy-turvy world of capitalism, this rational approach to crime is tipped over on its head. The legal system assumes quite the opposite, that poverty creates more choices. If the rich steal when they do not need to, the police and courts often assume, 'it is because of physical ill health, mental illness or evil influence'.[5]

The low income offender is more likely to be physically or mentally ill but has to take on individual responsibility for his offences and condition and is punished both for the crime and for being poor.

Crime: real, imagined and made up

THE REAL picture of crime is distorted, both coincidentally—in the gathering of statistics—and deliberately—to suit the ends of those who call for a stronger police force.

Much crime is not reported, very often because uninsured people see no point in doing so, or because it is dealt with by families or friends. As the PSI study points out, 'The police are the last resort in a long process of social control'.[6]

The police's version of crime is very different from the reality. They both exaggerate the seriousness of many crimes and play up the role that they can have in stopping it. Their stereotyping of criminals as a violent, identifiable section of the community is designed to downplay the economic roots of crime. In increasing fears of an 'enemy within' they make themselves look useful. This distorted picture is widely believed, thanks to the backing it gets in all forms of popular media.

One survey found that 43 percent of people fear burglars.[7] But the image of the typical burglar as a violent villain has little foundation in reality. In fact, 'the typical burglar is an unskilled, highly apprehensive teenager who is as keen to avoid confrontation as the householder'.[8]

We don't know about successful burglars, but we do know that of those caught by the police, in 1988 almost 9 percent were children between 10 and 14, one third were under 17 and 64 percent under 21.[9] The professional burglars who make a living from thieving are a tiny minority and violence is the last thing they want.

Burglaries are likely to be reported to the police when they involve violence. But even police statistics suggest the danger of violence from the burglar is exaggerated in popular fears. 157,400 burglaries and other offences involving entrance to buildings were reported in London in 1986. Only 399 involved some injury to victims and only 40 serious injury.[10]

Irrational fears are made worse by gutter journalism. One press report stated, 'In an extraordinarily large number of cases the inside of the house is deliberately defiled with urine or excreta by the thieves.'[11] In fact the 1983 British Crime Survey found, 'there was no reported incident occurring in the 11,000 householders interviewed of a burglar having soiled (urinated or defecated) over carpets and furniture and only a few incidents of deliberate damage.'[12]

For many people, particularly the old, burglary may be a horribly upsetting experience. But it is made worse by the portrayal of the burglar as a violent, crazed criminal who strikes in the dead of the night.

Robbery too is distorted. Street robbery involving serious violence is very infrequent. In 1989 17,315 robberies were recorded in London of which only 47 cases involved serious injury, with no fatalities.[13]

Robbery is distressing, but people's ability to deal with street thieves is undermined by the image of most robbers as violent thugs. The only point in creating such a myth is to justify the existence of violent police officers.

The most common characteristics of offenders are not professional villainy and self interest but poverty, isolation, boredom, an inability to cope, drink problems and mental illness.

Working class youth have always figured prominently in criminal statistics. Statistics of recorded crime in 1990 suggested that an increase in the number of young men in the population was associated with rises in all types of crime, particularly 'shop theft and criminal damage' but not with robbery.[14] The suggestion is that an increase in youth produces an increase in offences against property, not necessarily against people.

This doesn't mean that youths are not sometimes noisy, violent and anti social nuisances. Many working class people have real anxieties about the behaviour of their own adolescents. But the dangers of teenage violence are played up massively. Youth are not naturally brutal, senseless yobs. And, apart from the increased frustration of unemployment there is no reason to suppose that the youths of today are more anti social than they have ever been.

There are two major exceptions to the generalisation about the exaggeration of the menace of gangs of youths. One is joy riding in stolen cars. But as we have seen this danger is increased, not lessened, by high speed police chases. The second exception is violence by gangs of racist thugs. Yet this is precisely the type of collective violence which the police do nothing about, and even contribute to themselves.

The myth of the police holding society above a rising tide of threats from a demoralised part of the population has existed for as long as the police force.

The 'dangerous class' whom Victorian artists portrayed with animal faces were not scoundrels, drunkards and prostitutes but ordinary working people on low wages or in intermittent employment. Of course some of them committed crimes but there was no dangerous criminal class as such.

The attempt was made then to split off 'respectable' workers and make them hate and fear the poor. But it was as nonsensical in the nineteenth century to pretend Irish workers were all criminals as it is today to regard Black inner city youth as part of some marginal underclass.

Most offenders are neighbours, friends, workmates and relatives who for most of the time lead very ordinary dull lives. In the breaking of simple rules of social living offenders can create a great deal of distress for other people and themselves. They aren't working class heroes when they steal from their own or violently attack those near to them. Sometimes we can deal with them ourselves by showing disapproval, ridiculing, ostracising or demanding retribution.

True, we can't stop much crime under the present circumstances, but the police can do even less. Delinquencies are not reduced by the exercise of state violence by police, law courts and prisons. These institutions isolate, label and punish working class offenders and their families and their victims. They don't lessen the incidence of crime. When the penal system has done its worst, prisoners are thrown back into society more likely to be unemployed or homeless and even less able to cope.

The great apparatus of power built up around the police, all ostensibly to deal with crime, is of no help at all in protecting ordinary people.

Can they be reformed?—Labour's record

THE LABOUR PARTY accepts all the myths about police effectiveness in crime prevention. It has promised grants to owner-occupiers and tenants to keep out intruders, forgetting crime within the family.

It has promised, 'stronger locks, secure doors, vandal proof glass and more secure fencing'.[15] But such measures have been shown to merely deflect some crimes from one street to the next, increase people's fears and reinforce the stereotype of the criminal as some dangerous 'outsider'.

If Labour really wanted to make tower blocks less threatening and more hospitable it could put caretakers in every block. But this would cost money which Labour doesn't want to spend and give credence to the idea that more open communities, rather than bolted doors, could reduce some of the tensions and alienation which leads to crime.

Labour seeks cheap solutions to crime prevention because capitalism cannot deliver the real changes necessary. It's easier to purchase locks and bolts than to raise low incomes. Employing police is cheaper than building houses or reducing unemployment. College security guards and identity cards are cheaper than providing decent recreational facilities for students.[16] Labour has thus responded in recent years to 'law and order' campaigns by essentially copying the ideas of the establishment. Nevertheless, the party has a real problem when in comes to crime and policing.

The whole development of modern policing has been irrelevant to dealing with the types of crime which affect ordinary people. Riot training has not taken place because modern burglars have started using tear gas and plastic bullets, nor have housebreakers and petty thieves suddenly become more professional or more violent. Riot training cannot enable the police to deal with gangs of robbers or crowds of wife beaters.

When riot squads are sent against their real targets— pickets, inner city youths, demonstrators—and the real role of the police has become more obvious, then Labour politicians have often had to respond. The way they do this is not to argue against the police as thuggish defenders of the ruling class, but to say they are a neutral protective force which have been led astray by right wing politicians and police chiefs. What is needed, they say, is reform.

This idea was not a Labour Party invention. In 1962 the Royal Commission on the Police set up by a Conservative government noted that, 'the problem of the police, can... be restated as the problem of "controlling chief constables".'[17]

In opposition in the early 1980s the Labour Party called for measures, 'to ensure that we have a truly accountable police force... [and] effective democratic control by the community through its elected representatives'.[18]

Some local police authorities (made up of one third magistrates and two thirds councillors) tried to bring their own chief constables to book. What happened? The experience on Merseyside is illuminating.

Margaret Simey, chair of the Merseyside Police Authority, toiled for years to get the Home Office to grant some control of the police to the local authority. At one point it looked as though a tripartite structure for agreeing police policy had been set up consisting of the Home Office, local authority and police, with the local police authority being the 'centre of the web'.[19] In fact the Merseyside experience showed how impossible it was to make the police, 'more accountable within the existing system without challenging the doctrine of constabulary independence'.[20]

The police authority set up sub committees to check on police finance and complaints. It established liaison officers and community forums, hoping to subject the police to searching democratic scrutiny if not to actual control. But the community liaison became meaningless and the tripartite agreement disappeared like the Cheshire cat once class antagonisms became overt during the miners' strike of 1984-85. Only the grin of the chief constable remained as he spent £5 million in 20 weeks on police overtime without even consulting the police authority. As the chair of the police authority explained:

> When we passed a formal resolution asking him (the Chief Constable) to cease sending support units to the strike, he laughed out loud at us, and said he wasn't going to take any notice.[21]

Similarly, the attempt by the South Yorkshire police authority to stop the police using horses and dogs against striking miners was thwarted by a court ruling.

But couldn't the police be made accountable by a Labour government. Wasn't the problem in the miners' strike that left wing police authorities came up against the Tory government?

Even in the 'Golden Age' of Labour, the Attlee government of the post war years did not help workers' struggles. Labour used state forces against workers. As we have seen they didn't use the police in confrontations with strikers, they used the army as strike breakers instead. No Labour government has repealed the 1920 Emergency Powers Act which enables governments to use any means necessary to deal with national emergencies such as very large strikes[22] Central organisation set up to break a general strike, initially the Supply and Transport Committee, remained a permanent feature and was not dismantled by post war or subsequent Labour governments. This body is now known as the Civil Contingencies Unit.[23]

An attempt was made during the Labour government of 1974-1979 to give trade unionists clearer rights to picket. If the former Metropolitan Commissioner Robert Mark is to be believed, proposals to amend the law on picketing were made by Michael Foot but were blocked by the Association of Chief Police Officers. According to Mark,

> the Home Office arranged a meeting between representatives of all chief officers and Michael Foot's senior civil servants at which we left them in no doubt that the proposals would be publicly opposed by every chief officer. Happily they were abandoned and no harm was done.[24]

Labour claimed in 1987 that,

> Under the Tories the police have unwillingly been diverted from their proper role in preventing and detecting crime. Instead they have been pitched into social and industrial conflicts in a role alien to the traditions of good British policing.[25]

But it's not been much different under Labour. During the Wilson government there was the long and bitter Robert Arundels strike 1966-1968. During that strike there was heavy police violence. Compensation was won by some strikers who had been assaulted by the police.[26] MI5 was used against the seamen under the same government. Under the Callaghan Labour government there was mass picketing and police violence at Grunwicks. Stuart Weir, writing in **New Society**, described how the entrance was cleared on one occasion:

> Two phalanxes of police began to make a series of charges against the crowd... the people began to shout and scream in panic... People who had been thrown out of the picket

usually onto the ground were then punched, pushed or kicked right out of the way... on 7 November occurred some of the most violent clashes of the entire dispute... Many of those present thought the police themselves had caused most of the trouble, and a deputation of 3,000 marched to Willesden Green police station to protest. [27]

Allegations made against the police were denied by both them and the Labour home secretary. The police protected the fascists in the late 1970s and the Special Patrol Group killed Blair Peach under the same Labour government.[28]

At the root of the problem is the view in the Labour Party, on left as well as right, that the state is not some institution designed solely to protect class rule, but can be democratised, made neutral and forced to serve the interests of everyone.

This view means that Labour is even happy to *increase* police powers, arguing that they can be turned to the public good. Police numbers have regularly been increased under Labour. During Thatcher's government, Labour-controlled Metropolitan Counties increased police force strength, mobility, premises and technical equipment with hardly a murmur of protest. In a period of local spending cuts, they increased expenditure on police.[29] One of the claimed justifications for abolishing the Metropolitan Counties was their extravagance, but ironically much of that so called extravagance involved overspending on the police.

With the upsurge of class confidence and militancy in the miners' strike of 1984-85 sections of the Labour Party swung the party temporarily to the left on the question of the role of the police and strike breaking. At the Labour Party conference in 1984, 30 motions were tabled on the use of forces from other counties and police tactics.[30]

After a successful resolution highly critical of police action, Leslie Curtis, then chair of the Police Federation asked,

> how it would be possible for the police to serve in Britain in a crisis if the party in power forbade them to intervene to restore law and order and if the law breakers happened to be engaged in an industrial dispute?[31]

The police need not have worried. Neil Kinnock, leader of the Labour Party during the miners' strike, was desperate to condemn pickets and stand by the police. Similar sentiments were expressed by Labour leaders in the massive class struggles of the Great Unrest of 1910-1914.

Like Neil Kinnock they said 'a plague on both your houses' and described the violence of the struggle as 'the upper... and lower jaw of the same clinch'. In major class struggles the Labour Party, 'sides with the state and stands for the preservation of capitalist society'.[32] After the police smashed the last mass picket at Rupert Murdoch's Wapping fortress, injuring 300 people, Kinnock said he regarded the pickets as 'outcasts from the labour movement' who would get no support from him.[33]

Labour in opposition did promise in 1987 to repeal the 1984 Police and Criminal Evidence Act and replace it with an act which clearly defines police powers and citizens' rights.[34] Nevertheless, the Police and Criminal Evidence Act was largely based on the recommendations of a Royal Commission on Criminal Procedure set up by a Labour government. At the time of the Commission's Report the **Guardian** could comment:

> The difference between the Labour and Conservatives on the rights of suspects versus the needs of the police is one of emphasis rather than fundamental principle.[35]

Labour governments have also used the most despised powers of the secret state. In the 1970s Labour used the Official Secrets Act against the 'ABC' defendents Crispin Aubrey, Duncan Campbell and Jo Berry who 'had lifted only a small corner of the veil of secrecy' covering state surveillance.[36] When it came to the Zircon affair during the Thatcher government in which journalist Duncan Campbell publicised the expensive plans for a surveillance satellite never discussed in Parliament, Neil Kinnock's response was thin. The Labour leader attacked neither the secrecy nor the cost of the satellite but just,

> accused the government of incompetence in its failure to act effectively against the **New Statesman** magazine to prevent publication of material prejudicial to national security.[37]

What about community policing?

LABOUR LEADERS wish, like many of their supporters, to take the rough edges off the police, without in any way threatening their powers or their existence. They say they would like to root out police racism, to reduce the most overt attacks on pickets and demonstrators. They claim they would like to cut down police corruption.

The key, they argue, is that the police force should no longer be seen to be a force imposing rules on working class people from outside. Instead it should be accountable to and part of the community. This is one of the ways in which they hope the police can become 'firm but fair'. Neil Kinnock told the 1985 Labour conference: 'We want to put the state where it belongs in a democracy; not over the heads of the people, but under the feet of the people.'[38]

Labour politicians put 'the community' at the centre of many of their schemes, and none more so than with the police. 'Community' is an all purpose word that is never defined, but has a cosy democratic feel about it. In Labour's policy document on crime prevention, **Protecting our People**, the word 'community' is mentioned 13 times on the first three pages![39] They see the police as neutral, and they argue that potentially at least the whole of society is one large community in which all people have essentially the same interests. Therefore, to them, it makes sense to argue that the police can really be an impartial arbiter in the residual frictions in society.

This notion leaves aside the fact that by their very nature, the police under capitalism are a public power imposed from outside. It ignores too the fact that capitalism doesn't create communities, it breaks them down. Real communities exist where joint activities and decisions are made about the whole business of living. In capitalist societies so many aspects of control are taken away from workers. Real communities only exist when workers are organised to take some control over their lives as they do in times of struggle. The police, the courts, the prisons all exist as *external* public powers controlled by the class whose interests they serve.

Nevertheless, the idea of community policing has an aura of fairness and consideration which is plainly absent from the use of riot police and frame ups. In reality, however, community policing has no radical credentials and is often supported by those who are also in favour of the most heavy handed tactics in other situations. Often there has been little to separate Labour and

Tory views on the subject. For example:

> At a conference on community policing held at Exeter
> University in March 1982, unable to address the audience
> in person, Merlyn Rees, the former Labour Home Secretary,
> sent along instead a speech by William Whitelaw, his
> Conservative opposite number, to be read out as it exactly
> expressed his views.[40]

The former Chief Constable of Devon and Cornwall, John
Alderson, was in the 1980s one of the primary advocates of
community policing. For him the police could operate as
'activators of the good in society'. They were particularly well
suited to do this because of their 'unrivalled knowledge of crime
and social awareness.'[41] His idea of community policing was that
the police would act as a catalyst—the community would be
stimulated to help its self appointed moral leaders.[42] His vision
is based on an idyllic view of society which will ring no bells with
anyone living in Britain's cities. Community policing would,

> exist in its purest form when all the elements of the
> community both official and unofficial would conceive of the
> common good and combine to produce a social climate in an
> environment conducive of good order and the happiness of
> all those living within it.[43]

Understandably, Alderson stopped being a police chief and
became an aspiring Liberal politician instead.

At first glance there seemed to be a clear distinction between
officers like Alderson and the hard cops who sneer at the very
notion of community. Hard cops see themselves surrounded by
villains and chaos. For example, the Manchester Chief Constable, James Anderton, saw as his target 'social non-conformist
malingerers, idlers, parasites, spongers, frauds, cheats and
unrepentant criminals.'[44]

But the distinction is not as wide as it appears. Both versions
are about control. The 'alternatives' are in fact complementary
aspects of policing. Indeed, Alderson himself is steeped in both
traditions. Before becoming Chief Constable of Devon and
Cornwall, he held the post of Assistant Commissioner at Scotland
Yard where he,

> introduced weapons training, which included the L39A1

high velocity rifle and the Smith and Wesson Model 100 handgun. When he was commandant of the police staff college at Bramshill, he ran advisory courses on political subversion and control of demonstrations.[45]

Indeed after the 1981 riots many of the advocates of the toughest tactics accepted at least some of the arguments for community policing. The possibility of hard and soft tactics working in concert was spelled out by Alderson:

> In community policing... the flow of information improves. The negative attitudes of a community towards the criminal process turns positive... when in such a setting the police have to use force and to exercise their legal role they are better understood and in their turn far less alienated.[46]

What Alderson means is that whilst the police may use violence, their task of control is made much easier if they can also enlist the moral assent of at least some of the public. Consensus policing means that the police presence is tolerated or in some cases appreciated or actually demanded. Being acceptable on the streets was seen as fundamentally important at the very inception of the Metropolitan Police. The police officer, despised at the time by most people, should aim to be 'civil and obliging to all people of every rank and class.'[47]

This is all about gift wrapping a still violent force. Even the advocates of community policing want to have just 25 percent of police on the beat as opposed to the usual proportion of 1 or 2 percent.[48] And when conflict and class struggle mount these officers are expected to melt away as the hard cops step in. The rationale behind community policing was spelled out by the Labour Deputy Leader of Merseyside Council:

> If you read police literature you find that most forms of policing are pretty ineffective, so you might as well give the people what they want, which is police officers on the beat... I wanted to push beat policing not becuses it reduces crime but because it increases people's acceptance and confidence in the police.[49]

This idea is at the heart of Labour policy. It argues more police on the beat will create a better relationship between police and public.

However, the problem remains that few people are stupid enough not to notice the connection between the local police who they see day to day, and the forces that descend on them to snuff out any 'trouble making'. It is often assumed, for example, that because children have met one friendly officer then they will learn to love and respect all the rest. 'OK we know they're human but being a policeman rubs off on them'[50] was the pin-point accurate description of one Durham school student.

The PSI study found that the more contact people had with the police the less was their confidence in them:

> The police should be extremely cautious about adopting policies which would increase the amount of contact they have with people... it would be a brave person who would assert, from the findings of this study, that an increase in the number of encounters between the police and the public would improve the quality of police/public relations.[51]

The call for community policing suits the Labour leaders down to the ground as it appears to address the concerns of ordinary people while at the same time fitting in with what is actually a strategy developed by the more rational parts of the establishment.

Other people who want much more sincerely and thoroughly to reform the police end up in the same dead end as the Labour leaders. They are rightly outraged at the brutality and contempt shown to Blacks, the unemployed and other minorities, but then draw the wrong conclusion that such 'victims' are cut off from the working class as a whole. Class struggle, they argue, is incapable of taming the police, therefore reform from above is the only hope.

The role for ordinary people in this can come down to as little as, 'making demands on the police and carefully documenting criticism of their failures and political stances.'[52]

Many who want police reform also look to increasing the number of women and Blacks in the force as part of the solution. But we have already seen that the police behave as they do to protect the property and order of the rich, not because they are mostly male and White. Sections of the establishment, including the police, would like to see more Black officers as it would give the illusion of change.

Lord Scarman, reporting after the riots of 1981, looked to

controlling the inner cities through the creation of a Black middle class:

> Our underlying social strategy should be to create ethnic minority opportunities in the universities, the professions, the civil service, the police, in politics and public life, in business activities and in industrial management.[53]

The experience of the United States shows that such tactics have been invaluable in controlling without improving the inner cities, while the large scale recruitment of Black officers has done nothing to stop the police being a racist force.

People who want to reform the police, without changing the economic structure out of which it arises, end up having to hope that ideas and attitudes can be changed without challenging the system out of which they spring. One writer, Robert Reiner, has produced a very informative book on policing but reached strange conclusions. He accepted the minimal role of the police in crime prevention but wanted the useful service side of policing to be emphasised and for the left to stop attacking the police so that the force—through tactful management—would reform itself.[54] Margaret Simey, when chair of the Merseyside Police Authority, said that she needed 'a national will' to make the police more accountable. Others, having written interesting factual accounts of the police, seek equally mystical solutions:

> In general efforts to reverse the tide of repressive technology will succeed to the extent that the *civil libertarian reflex*, once so strong in this country, can be restored to vigour.[55]

The 'national will' could only be a meaningful concept in a society that was not divided into classes. Capitalism, however, is driven by the will of the ruling class to exploit and control the working class. Ultimately this means the police will only be reined in by the collective resistance of those they are sent to control.

Reform or revolution?

POLICE violence, racism, and sexism are embedded deep within the force. The police conform to the violence and bigotry of the rotten system they stand guard over. The state, of which the police force is a part, is the possession of a ruling class which willingly lets no part of it slip from its grasp.

The police, the army, the prisons and the court system are part of the machinery of class rule. Over 80 percent of high court judges are educated at public schools. As the courts are used against trade unions and the jury system is eroded, the class nature of the law has become more visible.

However, the state is not monolithic. The fraud of neutrality has to be maintained and occasionally with great publicity a rich man goes to prison or with less publicity a policeman is found guilty of a violent offence. Less well planned retreats, such as the release of the Tottenham Three and the Birmingham Six, show how campaigning can force concessions.

But the question remains for those who want more: how do we get it? Many, many people are horrified at the corruption and violence of the police and the legal system. Most, however, believe that in the last instance parliamentary democracy gives power to ordinary people which can be used to tame the police.

But parliament has never been allowed to override the decisions of those who really control the economy. The big companies and the City of London make investment decisions, open factories and close factories according to their own interests, not those of the government. Those who have had direct experience of the top echelons of the civil service, such as former Labour minister Tony Benn, testify that these people are loyal only to the rest of the ruling class. Time and again, army generals and police chiefs have scoffed at attempts by Labour politicians who have tried to curb their powers.

This is where real power lies in our society, with a ruling class. Its members have the power to make all the major decisions about society among themselves; elections are sideshows. The history of Labour governments shows that they become prisoners of the establishment, rather than its masters.

Labour politicians argue that it is neither necessary nor possible to do away with this set up, but there have been many examples this century that argue otherwise.

The state is not all powerful. The working class has the economic muscle and the potential strength and the numbers to smash it.

When workers rise in revolutionary struggle their numbers can defeat those forces which in periods of inactivity or isolated struggle seemed all powerful. State oppression, whatever the level of technology, depends on being able to deal with relatively small numbers at a time. When hundreds of thousands rise, the vulnerability of the most elaborate state machines becomes clear. The massive terror apparatus of the Shah of Iran and all his military hardware were not capable of preventing revolution in Iran in 1979.

As mass strikes gather momentum, capitalists face problems with their police. The question of arms becomes difficult. Rifles and heavy arms may be held in police stations but then police stations may be vulnerable to attack and the arms go into the workers' hands. Anyone who believes that the British ruling class has no fear of revolution should just examine the fortress design and strategic positioning of police stations built in the late 1970s and 1980s.

As demonstrations grow to hundreds of thousands, then police dispersal techniques become ineffective. What should the ruling class do? Does it issue the police with more arms and encourage them to kill rather than terrorise? Police are not normally trained to kill. Once the whole force is turned into a collective killing force then its usefulness as a buffer force becomes negligible and the whole myth about policing by consent is exploded.

In any successful revolution, sections of the state's forces change sides. This is different from saying the police are simply 'workers in uniform'. In all 'normal' times police officers stand firmly on the side of the bosses. In a revolutionary situation it can be different. Even state forces are affected by the magnitude and speed of the events. For example, sections of the French police in 1968 mutinied, as did the British police in 1918 and 1919. Police unionism spread in the US in the enormous strike wave of 1919.

Thus in the light of smaller struggles the police may appear to be an invincible state force; when the mass strike or the revolutionary situation gathers momentum then the police become more of an irrelevance and the army moves to the centre of the stage. But what of the army? If anything most soldiers are less imbued with a commitment to preserving the status quo than are police officers. They don't have the day to day experience of pushing people around to reinforce their commitment. They have been trained instead to deal with a much more distant enemy. They usually despise their officers even in normal times. In a revolutionary situation they can see the possibility of successful revolt. Soldiers, therefore, can and do mutiny—a key part of any successful revolution.

Such events create the possibility of a proper reckoning with the real powers in our society, of removing the need for a police force to keep us all in our places, and the chance for the first time ever to get to grips with the real roots of crime.

Conclusion

Fraud squad

WE STARTED out by aiming to measure the performance of the police against their stated aim of protecting everyone in society and their belongings. They have failed.

They have failed for two fundamental reasons. One is that the real roots of crime are buried deep in the structure of our society. The other reason is that the police are not really concerned with looking after ordinary people. Quite the opposite, they are interested in keeping ordinary people in their place in order to look after the interests of the tiny ruling class at the top of society. Let us review the results in a bit more detail.

The real roots of crime

ALL SOCIETIES that are divided into classes are based upon exploitation. Slave owners lived off the produce of slaves. Feudal lords lived from the labour of serfs. Capitalists depend for their own survival and the profits of their companies on the work carried out by their employees. Every one of these societies is at bottom based upon the theft of the labour power of the exploited classes.

However, the rules governing that theft have changed with different forms of society. In a slave owning economy even the very body of the slave was stolen from him or her and driven to work by coercion. Under capitalism, however, things stand differently. Legally, we have the right not to work for a boss. In practice, however, the bosses' monopoly over land, factories and resources means that we are compelled to work, or to hang around on the dole waiting to work.

Other rules govern the way in which capitalism operates. Capitalism is based upon ruthless competition. This can take the form of wars, piracy and plunder—which is the means by which British capitalism stole a lead from the rest in earlier centuries. More centrally, however, the competition revolves around the production of commodities. This doesn't make the struggle any less ruthless as workers are thrown on the dole, communities are wrecked and peasants are starved as the whirlwinds of competition wreak their havoc.

A common thread runs through all this. A ruling class which controls production everywhere demands that the law works in its favour. It demands that the flow of wealth that accrues to it because of its ownership of the factories, mines and offices should go on unimpeded. Any actions which might staunch or reverse the flow, such as strikes or theft from the rich, are to be attacked.

The ruling class is ruthless in exploiting those below it and savage in competition among itself, but it insists that this grabbing of wealth and resources must stop at its own boundaries. Therefore capitalism ensures that there will always be great need in society. It ensures the conditions that give rise to crime.

However, there is a contradiction at the heart of the relationship between class and crime in modern capitalism. Whilst capitalism defines crime and drives people towards it, most crimes are committed by the poor against the poor. Most crime is alienated behaviour forced on the most desperate in society—it is not a fightback against society.

This makes crime a serious issue, both to the lives of ordinary people, and for the political purposes of politicians and police chiefs. They argue that crime is committed by a malicious, morally weak section of the population who prey on otherwise happy communities and therefore need to be sorted out by a special force, the police. This argument gets a hearing among working class people and not just because it is repeated *ad nauseum*. It appears, most of the time, to fit with reality.

But we have seen how wrong this picture is of a 'criminal class' lurking among us. Whether the police's stereotypical criminal is an Irish worker, as it was in the nineteenth century; a young black person, as it often is today; or perhaps just a less defined collection of individuals, it has always been misplaced.

Huge numbers of very ordinary people are driven to commit crimes from time to time. Very few motorists could claim to have never broken the driving laws. In the early 1990s ten million people simultaneously committed the politically and economically motivated offence of not paying the poll tax. Less trivial offences are also committed on a fairly random basis. Most burglaries and street thefts are not carried out by professional criminals.

The only factor correlating with the tendency to commit crime is social deprivation. Working class youth are more likely to burgle, and the youth of the poorest section of the working class are even more likely to do it.

Similarly, the most serious crimes of violence and sexual assault are overwhelmingly committed by ordinary people. The vast majority of assaults and murders take place in the home or among people who know each other. The people who perpetrate these crimes are not a select band of professionals who make it their business to beat people up (unlike the police). These are unexceptional people whose crowded, dingy conditions make them crack from time to time. The same factors bear on the incidence of rape. This is not, by and large, committed by strangers, but by people known to the victim whose alienation from society—plus the images of women that are encouraged by our society—drives them to commit such a terrible crime.

Capitalism has created a situation in which most people's wants and needs are not fulfilled. We live on meagre wages and in substandard housing, while at the same time we are bombarded with images of wealth and the 'virtues' of greed and desire.

Still, most working class people don't commit anything other than the most trivial crimes. They don't burgle each other's houses or pick each other's pockets. They struggle by, they have a sense of solidarity with each other that doesn't come from the rantings of police chiefs, but is a basic product of working class experience. The vast bulk of the working class fight for what they get, but they fight in an organised fashion against the bosses rather than amongst themselves.

Within the working class, however, there are pools of people to whom such solutions seem irrelevant. They have been driven beyond any collective answer by their alienation and turn instead to the individual escape of crime. This pool grows and contracts with the general state of the economy. But the fact that it is economic misery and alienation that causes crime is borne out powerfully by statistics showing deprivation and the incidence of crime rising and falling in near-unison.

What do the police do about it?

THE INEFFICIENCY of the police in stopping or solving crime is stunning. An estimated national clear up rate of less than 2 percent of all thefts from the person is pathetic. Given that accidental discovery of information might be supposed to reveal the identity of one thief out of fifty, then every one of us probably knows as much about who steals as does the average police officer.[1]

All the evidence also points to the fact that any increase in police numbers has no effect on solving crime. The only outcome of there being more police is that they 'discover' more crimes having taken place around them.

These figures blow a hole in the police myth, but they should not really be surprising. Crimes take place all the time and in all places, generated by the failings of our society. The police cannot deal with them because they are not up to patching over all the problems created by capitalism.

In any case, the police are not designed to fulfil this role at all. They defend the property and lives of the rich, not the poor. They penetrate working class communities, go after thieves, ask questions in order to better know those who might individually threaten the interests of the rich, and, as importantly, so as to be in a position to deal with collective outbursts of anger when they occur.

We have seen how, historically, the police force was developed to deal with a specific problem thrown up by capitalism. The working class is too powerful to be held in check by brute force alone—therefore something less cumbersome than the army is needed. On the other hand, coercion cannot be neglected altogether, therefore the police need to be on hand to break up pickets and demonstrations when necessary. The balance between persuasion and coercion has swung back and forward over time, but the police's central role as a body at the disposal of the ruling class has not changed.

The police have themselves furnished the best possible illustration of how they see fit to deploy their resources, and therefore what they see as their real job. A diary of the occasions on which over 1,000 officers were turned out in London in 1986

Table 10. Large police engagements 1986

Date	Event	Number
22 February	Picket at Wapping	1,109
24 February	March and meeting	1,153
1 March	Wapping	1,123
8 March	Wapping	1,117
29 March	Wapping	1,169
5 April	Wapping	1,202
6 April	March (Wapping)	2,148
12 April	Wapping	1,185
19 April	Wapping	1,185
19 April	CND demo	1,611
26 April	Wapping	1,146
3 May	March (Wapping)	1,445
10 May	Wapping	1,037
24 May	Wapping	1,034
31 May	Wapping	1,034
31 May	Queen's birthday	3,471
7 June	Wapping	1,032
28 June	Anti Apartheid march	2,649
1 July	West German state visit	1,714
20 July	Anti racist march	1,231
23 July	Royal wedding	2,907
24 July	Drugs raid, Brixton	1,342
24 August	Notting Hill Carnival	3,899
25 August	Notting Hill Carnival	4,918
9 November	Remembrance Day	1,907
6 December	State opening of Parliament	1,593
31 December	New Year, Trafalgar Square	1,719

was contained in that year's chief constable's annual report.[2]

It showed that over 20 percent of all police available in London at the time were sent: to defend Rupert Murdoch's scab print plant on 12 occasions; to keep six demonstrations in line; to clear the way three times for the royal family; to honour the West German president and mark the carnage of the First and Second World Wars; to raid an estate and to keep an eye on three days' worth of celebrations.

The police don't protect ordinary people from crime because they can't and they don't want to. Their real job is to help hold together a system that creates crime.

Is there an alternative?

IF THE police have no real role in preventing the crimes that affect ordinary people, what can be done? The simple answer is to remove the conditions which create crime in the first place. This means dealing with the inequality, the need and the alienation generated by our society.

But the police, along with the rest of the state, stand guard over the present society, rebuking all attempts to make fundamental changes through 'the democratic process'. Only the most superficial and transitory reforms are allowed past them.

In a real democracy—under socialism—people would have equal access to resources. Preventing crime and disorder would be the business of everyone. The mass of people would be trusted with running their own lives for the first time. Under such a set-up, with mass participation and different aims, we could really start to deal with the crimes suffered by ordinary people.

The rationale for the vast majority of crime would turn to dust. Small scale property crime only exists because capitalism denies property to most of us. Shoplifting would become an irrational exercise when people have access to their needs.

Seemingly more intractable crimes could be progressively sorted out. Violence against women would be taken seriously for the first time. The privatised world of distorted personal relationships in which so much of it takes place would be opened up and be the concern of everyone.

A solution would not come immediately, but the 'muck of ages' would be progressively thrown off as men and women struggle together against oppression of every kind. The alienation and sexual repression forced on us by capitalism could be overcome.

George Orwell saw glimpses of such a transformation when workers seized power in Barcelona in 1936. Patrols did not hound beggars. There was no reason as, 'The usual beggars had disappeared, taken care of by the union's welfare system.'[3] Moreover, 'Human beings were trying to behave as human beings ... a state of affairs worth fighting for.'[4]

In the miners' struggles of 1984-85, communites were created which had far higher standards of solidarity than before the strike. During the Paris Commune in 1870,

> there were no more corpses in the morgue, no nocturnal burglaries, scarcely any robberies. In fact for the first time since the days of February 1848 the streets of Paris were safe and that without police of any kind.[5]

After the police were ejected from Derry in 1969,

> petty crime was handled by the Free Derry police which was independent of both IRAs. Tony O'Doherty who had temporarily given up a career as an international footballer... was engaged as a police chief. His personal popularity had a lot to do with the fact that after a few weeks there was no petty crime. Shop owners in the Creggan reported that for the first time since they had set up in business they could lock up at night with an easy mind.[6]

If real communities are created then real community control can be exerted without calling in any outside force. This does not mean to say that under socialism crime will just disappear, but it does mean that all sorts of methods of control could be adopted which would be directly embodied in everyday life.

Marriage would not be a property arrangement nor would children be 'owned' by their parents. There would be escape from the iron ring of family tensions. The development of individual potential would be enormous. Areas of present policing currently regarded as 'rubbish' work by the police such as traffic safety and lost children or property would be far better performed by workers committed to really helping out. Dealing with domestic emergencies would be a priority, as would finding alternative accommodation, dealing with natural disasters, pollution of all types, unsafe work premises and medical attention for those caught in accidents or fires.

Above all, the source of crime in poverty and alienation could be properly tackled for the first time as economic problems are sorted out and the bulk of the population takes control over running their own lives and society. As Frederick Engels argued over a hundred years ago:

> freed from capitalist slavery, from the untold horrors, savagery, absurdities and infamies of capitalist exploitation, people will gradually become accustomed to the observation of the elementary rules of social life... they will become accustomed to obeying them, without force, without compulsion, without subordination.[7]

The present 'law and order' is class order involving injustice, unnecessary suffering, gross inequality, fraud and violence. In the construction of a new social order there will be conflict and thousands of problems to sort out, but they can be tackled once the economic chaos is ended and the world set on its feet.

Notes

Introduction

1. **Guardian,** 4 September 1991.
2. David J Smith, **Police and People in London,** vol. 1, Policy Studies Institute no. 618, London 1983, pp. 299-300.
3. See chapter 2 for details.

1. Violence and Society

1. **Report of the Commissioner of Police of the Metropolis 1986,** Cm 389, London 1987, p. 1.
2. **Criminal Statistics England and Wales 1988,** Cm 847, London 1989, table 4.2, p. 74.
3. Ibid., p. 67.
4. Ibid., p. 76.
5. Ibid., para 4.5, p. 69.
6. David J Smith and Jeremy Gray, **Police and People in London,** vol. 4, Policy Studies Institute no. 621, London 1983, p. 64.
7. **Observer,** 2 November 1986.
8. Ibid.
9. **Report of the Commissioner of Police of the Metropolis 1986,** p. 78.
10. **Observer,** 22 May 1988.
11. Barry Poyner and Caroline Ward, **Preventing Violence to Staff,** The Tavistock Institute of Human Relations, para. 298.
12. Ibid., para. 123.
13. Ibid., p. 1.
14. **Racial Attacks. Report of a Home Office Study,** London 1981, p. 11.
15. **Observer,** 14 May 1989.

16. Ibid.
17. Ibid.
18. **Observer**, 14 May 1989.
19. Simon Field, **Trends in Crime and their Interpretation**. Home Office Research Study 119, London 1990, p. 47.
20. Robert Storch, 'The Plague of Blue Locusts', in Mike Fitzgerald, Gregor McLennan and Jennie Pawson, eds., **Crime and Society**, London 1981, p. 105.
21. **Observer**, 26 June 1988. My emphasis.
22. Melissa Benn and Ken Worpole, **Death in the City**, Canary Press 1986, p. 6.
23. **Report of the Commissioner of Police of the Metropolis 1989**, Cm 1070, London 1990, p. 61. This excluded the 115 deaths 'in police care' when the police were breaking the ambulance workers' strike.
24. **Report of HM Chief Inspector of Constabulary 1988**, HC 449, London 1989, p. 111; **Report of the Commissioner of Police of the Metropolis 1989**, p. 61.
25. **Report of HM Chief Inspector of Constabulary 1988**, tables 9.1, 9.2, pp. 70, 71.
26. Table 11. Notifiable offences recorded by the police in which firearms were reported to have been used in England and Wales:

	Air guns	Other guns	Total
1985	6,380	3,362	9,742
1986	5,886	3,477	9,363
1987	5,172	3,830	9,002

In 1987 air guns were reported to have caused 2,203 injuries, compared for 421 for other firearms. **Criminal Statistics England and Wales 1987**, London 1988, Tables 3.5, 3.9, 3.10. See also **Sunday Times**, 23 January 1983.
27. An interesting but difficult piece of research which hasn't yet been done could look at the proportion of extremely violent offenders who had been trained in violence either by the police or the army.
28. **Annual Abstract of Statistics 126 1987**, London 1990, p. 72, table 3.35; **Criminal Statistics England and Wales 1987**, CM 498, London 1988, p. 61; **Report of the Commissioner of Police of the Metropolis 1987**, CM 389, London 1988, p. 91; **Report of HM Chief Inspector of Constabulary 1987**, HC 521, London 1988, p. 40.
29. 'Report of the Commissioner of Police of the Metropolis 1963'; **PP 63/64 XVIII**, London 1964, p. 35. In 1963 7,598 police were injured in sports and games as compared with only 3,028 assaulted on duty.
30. **Report of HM Chief Inspector of Constabulary 1988**, HC 449,

London 1989, pp. 45, 46.

31. David J Smith, **Police and People in London**, vol. 3, Policy Studies Institute no. 620, London 1983, p. 29.
32. See **Report of the Commissioner of Police of the Metropolis 1983**, CM 9268, London 1984.
33. **Report of the Commissioner of Police of the Metropolis 1986**, p. 50.
34. **Report of the Commissioner of Police of the Metropolis 1989**, p. 23. For further information see also Benn and Worpole, op cit., p. 72.
35. **Report of the Commissioner of Police of the Metropolis 1989**, calculated from table 7.4, p. 23.
36. Smith and Gray, op cit., pp. 51, 53.
37. Benn and Worpole, op cit., p. 65.
38. Ronald Clark and Mike Hough, **Crime and Police Effectiveness**, Home Office Research Study no. 797, London 1984, p. 8; Benn and Worpole, op cit., p. 67.

2. Crime: fact and fiction

1. **Criminal Statistics England and Wales 1988**, CM 847, London 1989; table 2.11, p. 40. Excluded from the percentages are cases where nothing was stolen or the value of property was not known. These are recorded offences only but it is reasonable to assume that the unreported burglaries will tend to involve relatively small sums.
2. **Report of the Commissioner of Police of the Metropolis 1986**, CM 158, London 1987, p. 47.
3. Ronald Clark and Mike Hough, **Crime and Police Effectiveness**, Home Office Research Study no. 797, London 1984. p. 7.
4. **Audit**, The Journal of AGB Research Limited, Gazette, London Spring 1979, p. 4.
5. **Guardian**, 13 November 1981.
6. Ibid., 27 September 1984; see also Trevor Bennett and Richard Wright, **Burglars on Burglary**, Aldershot 1984.
7. **Report of the Commissioner of Police of the Metropolis 1986**, p. 73.
8. **Guardian**, 11 May 1988.
9. Ibid.
10. Clark and Hough, op cit., p. 8.
11. Ibid., p. 6.
12. **Criminal Statistics England and Wales 1988**, tables 2.11, 2.13, pp. 37, 42.
13. **Report of the Commissioner of Police of the Metropolis 1989**,

CM 1070, London 1990, table 17.2, p. 117.

14. **Report of HM Chief Inspector of Constabulary 1988**, HC 449, London 1990, Appendix 6, table 4.1, p. 105.
15. **Observer**, 13 July 1986.
16. **Criminal Statistics England and Wales 1988**, London 1989, tables 2a, 2.8, 2.9, 2.10, 2.15.
17. **Observer**, 8 December 1991.
18. Ernest W Pettifer, **The Court Resumes**, Bradford 1945, pp. 130, 131.
19. **Report of the Commissioner of Police of the Metropolis 1989**, table 17.2, p. 117.
20. **Times**, 25 March 1982.
21. Clark and Hough, op cit., p. 10.
22. Ibid.
23. David J Smith, **Police and People in London**, vol. 3, Policy Studies Institute no. 620, London 1983, p. 36.
24. Robert Reiner, **The Politics of the Police**, Brighton 1985, pp. 147-148.
25. **Criminal Statistics England and Wales 1988**, table 2a.
26. **Times**, 25 March 1982.
27. Similarly in the early 1970s an investigation into crime in New York showed an under-reporting of robberies because new police commissioner Patrick Murphy 'had placed far more emphasis on linking promotion to crime control than did his predecessor'. **Guardian**, 16 May 1972.
28. **Times**, 25 March 1982.
29. **Criminal Statistics England and Wales 1988**, para. 2.20.
30. L Blom Cooper and R Drabble, 'Police Perception of Crime', **British Journal of Criminology**, London 1982, pp. 184-7.
31. David J Smith, **Police and People in London**, vol. 1, Policy Studies Institute no. 618, London 1983, p. 38.
32. Smith, **Police and People in London**, vol. 3, op cit., p. 34.
33. David J Smith and Jeremy Gray, **Police and People in London**, vol. 4, Police Studies Institute 1983, p. 521.
34. Robert Storch, 'The Plague of Blue Locusts', in Mike Fitzgerald, Gregor McLennan and Jennie Pawson, eds., **Crime and Society**, London 1981, p. 93.

3. Class and corruption

1. **Guardian**, 17 May 1974; **Sunday Times**, 16 January 1983.
2. Keith Dean, 'Tax evasion, criminality and sentencing the tax offender', **British Journal of Criminology**, London January 1981, p. 57.

3. **Enforcement of the Law Relating to Social Security**, report of NACRO working party, London 1986, p. 71. Emphasis added in NACRO report.
4. **Report of the Committee on Abuse of Social Security Benefits**, Cmd 5228, London 1973, para. 437, p. 205.
5. NACRO, op cit., pp. 48, 70.
6. **Financial Times**, 22 September 1975.
7. Ibid., 26 February 1980.
8. **Guardian**, 24 October 1985.
9. Ibid., 28 September 1986.
10. Ibid., 12 March 1980.
11. **Financial Times**, 29 September 1989.
12. **Guardian**, 30 January 1986.
13. **Hansard**, 27 March 1986, col. 550; quoted in **Labour Research**, vol. 75, no. 9, London 1986.
14. **Times**, 22 September 1975.
15. Hank Messick and Burt Goldblatt, **The Mobs and the Mafia**, London 1973, p. 203.
16. **Guardian**, 24 July 1986.
17. Ibid., 16 April 1988.
18. Ibid., 17 December 1984.
19. **Sunday Times**, 19 July 1981.
20. Ibid., 12 July 1981.
21. Norman Skelhorn, **Public Prosecutor: The Memoirs of Sir Norman Skelhorn**, Bromley 1981, p. 65.
22. Ibid., p. 82.
23. **Report of HM Chief Inspector of Constabulary 1987**, London 1988, p. 101.
24. Ibid., table 4.5, p. 99.
25. Barry Cox, John Shirley and Martin Short, **The Fall of Scotland Yard**, Harmondsworth 1977, pp. 86, 87.
26. **Guardian**, 20 September 1976.
27. Ibid., 3 June 1980.
28. **Sunday Times**, 30 June 1974.
29. **Guardian**, 23 September 1986.
30. **Observer**, 30 March 1980.
31. A Henman, R Lewis, and T Malyos, **Big Deal. The Politics of the Illicit Drugs Business**, London 1985, p. 9.
32. **Guardian**, 21 March 1985.
33. Ibid., 8 January 1986, 13 September 1986, 26 September 1986.
34. Ibid., 25 November 1986.
35. **Sunday Times**, 13 December 1981.
36. Edwin Chadwick, 'Preventive Police', **London Review**, vol. 1, London 1835, p. 304.
37. **Guardian**, 15 October 1985; Ibid., 30 October 1985.

38. **Observer**, 5 May 1991.
39. Cox et al., op cit., p. 158.
40. Stephen Knight, **The Brotherhood Panther**, London 1985, p. 76.
41. **Times**, 8 August 1972.
42. **Guardian**, 6 January 1975.
43. Knight, op cit., p. 50.
44. Cox et al., op cit., p. 213.
45. **Guardian**, 21 July 1982.
46. Ibid.
47. Here another curious event can be mentioned. There was a similar attempted clean up in Paris in 1986: 'Nearly all the Paris crime squad undercover cars were neatly parked yesterday in the courtyard of the police headquarters. Top detectives are on an unofficial go slow protesting against accusations that cops have become robbers.' **Guardian**, 27 January 1986.
48. **Guardian**, 26 July 1982.
49. Ibid., 24 October 1989.

4. Bread and batons

1. Frederick Engels, **The Condition of the Working Class in England**, London 1969, p. 253.
2. Beatrice Webb, **English Local Government, English Poor Law History**, London 1927, p. 403.
3. Leon Radzinowitz, **A History of Criminal Law**, London 1948, vol. 3, p. 232.
4. Ibid., vol. 1, p. 1.
5. Ibid., p. 426 for details.
6. Douglas Hay, Peter Linebough, John G Rule, EP Thompson and Cal Winslow, **Albion's Fatal Tree. Crime and Society in Eighteenth Century England**, Harmondsworth 1977, p. 18.
7. Radzinovitz, op cit., vol. 4, pp. 121, 122.
8. Ibid., p. 123.
9. Paul Foot, **Red Shelley**, London 1984, p. 36.
10. Hay et al., op cit., p. 50.
11. SE Finer, **The Life and Times of Sir Edwin Chadwick**, London 1952, p. 179.
12. Quoted in TA Critchley, **A History of Police in England and Wales 900-1966**, London 1967, p. 47.
13. Robert Storch, 'The Plague of Blue Locusts, in Mike Fitzgerald, Gregor McLennan and Jennie Pawson, eds., **Crime and Society**, London 1981, p. 92.
14. Critchley, op cit., p. 51.

15. Charles Reith, **A New Study of Police History**, Harlow 1956, p. 156.
16. Ibid., p. 155.
17. RG Gammage, **History of the Chartist Movement 1837-1854**, London 1969, p. 132.
18. Ibid., p. 51.
19. Speech by John Fielding at Manchester. Ibid., p. 61.
20. Reith, op cit., p. 160.
21. Gammage, op cit., pp. 20, 23, 113, 116.
22. Ibid., p. 136.
23. Ibid., p. 133.
24. Storch, op cit., pp. 101-2.
25. Critchley, op cit., p. 95.
26. Ibid., p. 97.
27. Ewart W Clay, ed., **The Leeds Police 1836-1974**, Leeds n.d., p. 22.
28. Gammage, op cit., p. 296.
29. Ibid., p. 295.
30. Note the sentences placed on the agricultural workers by the Special Courts of Commission set up in the south of England in the early 1830s—six men and boys were hanged, 457 transported and 400 imprisoned with hard labour. JL Hammond and Barbara Hammond, **The Village Labourer 1760-1832**, London 1920, p. 284.
31. Dorothy Thompson, **The Chartists. Popular Politics in the Industrial Revolution**, Aldershot 1986, p. 86.
32. Storch, op cit., p. 95.
33. Gammage, op cit., p. 115.
34. David J Smith, **Police and People in London**, vol. 1. Policy Studies Institute no. 618, London 1983.
35. Leon Radzinovicz and Roger Hood, **A History of Criminal Law**, vol. 5, London 1986, p. 34.
36. Ibid., p. 343.
37. SE Finer, **The Life and Times of Sir Edwin Chadwick**, London 1952, p. 126.
38. 'The Charter. 24 March 1839'; quoted in ibid., p. 176.
39. Carolyn Steedman, **Policing the Victorian Community**, London 1984, pp. 57-8.
40. Ibid.
41. John English and Robert Houghton, **Summonses and Charges** (third revised edition), London 1980, p. 206.
42. Radzinovicz, op cit., vol. 3, p. 238.
43. EP Thompson, **The Secret State**, State Research Pamphlet no. 1, May 1979, p. 8.
44. Royden Harrison, **Before the Socialists**, London 1965, p. 119.
45. Ibid., p. 119.
46. **Marx and Engels on Britain**, Beijing 1953, p. 422.

47. Ibid., p. 424.
48. Eye witness account. See Henry Broadhurst MP, **From a Stonemasons Bench to the Treasury Bench,** London 1901, pp. 35-37.
49. Ibid., pp. 39-40.
50. Ibid., p. 40.
51. **Times**, 2 May 1867.
52. Ibid.
53. Harrison, op cit., p. 94.
54. Ibid., p. 136.
55. The split between the two can be seen very clearly in the fact that a big coal owner could use the police against his miners on the picket line and at the same time stand as a Liberal candidate for parliament on a policy of security for trade union funds and the ballot. The Liberal candidate was a Mr Lancaster, chairman of the Wigan Coal and Iron company. Ibid., p. 167.
56. Donald C Richter, **Riotous Victorians**, London 1981, p. 159.
57. Beatrice and Sidney Webb, **History of Trade Unionism**, London, p. 746.
58. Ibid., pp. 83, 199.
59. These model unions created a prototype of the later welfare state. They also attempted to control the supply of labour, operated emigration schemes, conducted education classes and collected unemployment statistics. The first industrial dispute statistics collected by central government were done at the Board of Trade by an ex trade union officer, John Burnett.
60. Webbs, op cit., p. 27.
61. 'Final report of Trade Union Commission', **PP 1868/1869 XXXI**, paras. 337, 338.
62. Webbs, op cit., p. 284.
63. Metropolitan and Constabulary police 1856-1887. Taken from **PP 1876 XXXIV**, pp. 105, 194, 327; **PP 1886 XXXIV**, p. 343; **PP 1890 XXXVI**, pp. 307, 555, 455; **PP 1894 XLII**, pp. 210, 217, 218, 221.
64. 'Eighth Report of Commission on Trade Unions', **PP XXXIX**, p. 345 para. 16070.
65. Ibid., p. 345, para. 16065.
66. **PP 1889 LXX**, p. 705.
67. Ibid., pp 42-3; Terry McCarthy, **The Great Dock Strike 1889**, Weidenfeld and Nicolson 1988, p. 42.
68. **Times**, 22 August 1889.
69. Ibid., 23 August 1889.
70. **Manchester Guardian**, 30 August 1889.
71. **Times**, 24 August 1889.
72. **Manchester Guardian**, 29 August 1889.
73. **Times**, 26 August 1889.

74. Ibid.
75. 'Report of the Commission of Police of the Metropolis 1889', **PP1890/91**, p. 333.
76. Ibid.
77. H Hendrick, **The Leeds Gas Strike 1890**, reprinted from **Miscellany**, vol. 16, publication of the Thoresby Society, Leeds 1979, pp. 88, 89.
78. John Gorman, **To Build Jerusalem**, London 1980, p. 20.
79. Taken from 'Reports of Inspectors of Constabulary' and 'Reports of Commissioners of Police of the Metropolis' for the appropriate years: **PP 1890 XXXVI**, pp. 309, 455, 555; **PP 1894 XLII**, p. 310; **PP 1896 XLII**, pp. 225, 318; **PP 1898 XLVI**, pp. 237, 332; **PP 1906 XLIX**, pp. 198, 203, 207; **PP 1907 XXXVI**, p. 26; **PP 1908 LXXXXIX**, pp. 834, 839, 843; **PP 1909 LXXII**, p. 886; **PP 1910 LXXV**, p. 700; **PP 1914-16 XXXII**, p. 133; **PP 1911 LXV**, p. 294; **PP 1913 LII**, pp. 663, 796; **PP 1914 LXVII**, p. 796.

    Calculations for each of constabulary figures 1887-1907 from totalling Districts 1, 2 and 3. For 1908-1913 by totalling Counties and Boroughs. All calculations for regular authorised police include the Metropolitan Police figures and dockyards police but exclude the City police and additional police outside London.

    References for workers involved in strikes taken to the nearest thousand from **PP 1889 LXX**, 'Reports on the strike and lockout of 1888', p. 705, by the Labour Correspondent of the Board of Trade J Burnett; **PP 1890 LXVIII**, p. 476; **PP 1890/1 LXVIII**, p. 404; **PP 1893/4 LXXXIII**; **PP 18984 LXXXI**

    'Reports on strikes and lockouts and on conciliations and Arbitration Boards in the UK in 1911', **PP 1912/3**, pp. 230-1; **PP 1914 XIVIII**, p. 363; **PP 1914/16 XXXVI**, pp. 492, 500.
80. **PP 1914/16 XXXII**, p. 191.
81. The same Macready was subsequently put in charge of the combined police and army operation during the Irish war of 1919-21.
82. Table 12. Metropolitan Police and Constabulary 1858-1978.

Year	Metropolitan	Constabulary
1858	6,276	12,653
1888	14,261	21,764
1918	22,176	35,536
1948	18,740	48,714
1978	26,589	90,057

The Metropolitan Police is controlled directly from the Home Office. Until the 1930s it represented a very high proportion of the total police in the country. Establishment figures are used and police women and City police are omitted in order to get a continuous set of statistics. See **PP 1876 XXXIV; PP 1890 XXXVI; PP 1920 XXII,** p. 493; **PP 1948 XIX; PP 1979/80 XII.**

Figure 8. Metropolitan and Constabulary size.

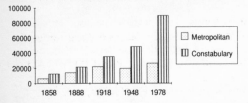

83. Cd 5568, Home Office Colliery Strike and Disturbances in Soiuth Wales Correspondance and Report, London November 1910 (**PP 1911 LXIV**), p. 35.
84. Ibid., p. 35.
85. Ibid., p. 48.
86. Ibid., p. 31.
87. Sir Neville Macready, **Annals of an Active life**, vol. I, London n.d., p. 137.
88. The 1867 commission, whilst recommending that combinations should be legal, wanted to exempt the railway workers from the provisions of the bill and in that industry wanted a month's notice of strikes. 'Final Report of the Trade Union Commission', **PP 1868/69 XXXI**, p. 339. The railway companies of the nineteenth century employed their own police who had heavy truncheons. See Mervyn Mitton, **The Policeman's Lot**, London 1985, p. 43.
89. Webbs, op cit., , p. 523.
90. Gorman, op cit. The romance of steam was bloody: between 1875 and 1899 12,870 men were killed at work and 68,575 injured. Ibid., p. 35.
91. Macready, op cit., p. 164.
92. Gorman, op cit., p. 92.
93. Macready, op cit., p. 163.
94. Tony Cliff and Donny Gluckstein, **The Labour Party: a Marxist History**, London 1988, pp. 55-6.
95. Ibid., p. 65.
96. Webbs, op cit., p. 539.
97. Ibid., p. 543.
98. Roger Geary, **Policing Industrial Disputes 1893-1985**, London 1985, p. 51.
99. Ibid., p. 52.
100. Tony Cliff and Donny Gluckstein, **Marxism and Trade Union Struggle. The General Strike of 1926**, London 1986, p. 204.
101. A similar situation arose in the Swedish general strike of 1909

when trade union bureaucrats supplied some specials to police the strike. Tony Cliff, 'Patterns of the Mass Strike', **International Socialism**, 2.29, London 1985, p. 7.

102.'Report of HM Chief Inspector of Constabulary for 1926', **PP 1927 XI**, p. 7.

103.Gorman, op cit., p. 127.

104.Keith Jeffrey and Peter Hennessy, **States of Emergency**, London 1983, p. 169.

105.Returns relating to the Metropolitan Police, **PP 1867 LVII**, p. 819.

106.Dorothy Thompson, op cit., p. 322.

107.Inspector of Constabulary report, **PP 1927 XI**, p. 7.

108.Jeffrey and Hennessy, op cit., p. 37.

109.Cab 23/7 Aug 18 1919 WC67.

110.**PP 1932/33 XV**, pp. 24-5.

111.Geary, op cit., p. 48.

112.'Report of the Committee on the Police Service of England Wales and Scotland (Desborough)', London 1920, **PP 1920 XXII**, p. 22.

113.Critchley, op cit., p. 96.

114.Gorman, op cit,. p. 51.

115.Tom Bowden, **Beyond the Limits of the Law**, Harmondsworth 1978, p. 239.

116.Ibid., p. 129.

5. Class traitors

1. Tony Cliff and Donny Gluckstein, **Marxism and Trade Union Struggle. The General Strike of 1926**, London 1986, p. 205.

2. Chanie Rosenberg, **1919, Britain on the Brink of Revolution**, London 1987, p. 23.

3. Anthony Judge and Gerald W Reynolds, **The Night the Police Went on Strike**, London 1968, p. 61.

4. Ibid., p. 70.

5. Ibid., p. 116.

6. Sir Neville Macready, **Annals of an Active Life**, vol. II, London 1956, p. 362.

7. Stuart Bowes, **The Police and Civil Liberties**, London 1966, p. 22.

8. Ibid., p. 22.

9. Judge and Reynolds, op cit., p. 160.

10. Ibid., p. 86. In that same year police were forming unions in 37 US cities and within weeks of the British police strikes came a similar strike in Boston.

11. 'Report of the Committee appointed to inquire into the cases of men dismissed from police and prison service on account of the 1919

strike', **PP 1924/5 XV**, para. 65, p. 25.
12. Judge and Reynolds, op cit., p. 233.
13. Ibid., p. 235.
14. Ibid., p. 233.
15. Ibid., p. 234.
16. Bowes, op cit., p. 22.
17. Charles Reith, **A New Study of Police History**, Harlow 1956, p. 146.
18. TA Critchley, **A History of Police in England and Wales 900-66**, London 1967, p. 52.
19. Judge and Reynolds, op cit., pp. 216, 224.
20. **PP 1890/91 LXVIII**, p. 691.
21. 'Report of the Committee on the Police Service of England, Wales and Scotland (Desborough)', London 1920, **PP 1920 XXII**, pp. 23-5.
22. 'Committee on Temporary Reductions from Police Pay'. **PP 1924-5 XV**, p. 3, para 3.
23. 'Police Pay (new entrants) Report', London 1933, **PP 1932-33 XV**, p. 5.
24. Ben Whittaker, **The Police in Society**, London 1979, p. 59.
25. **PP 1932/33 XV**.
26. 'Police Pay (new entrants) Report', op cit., p. 6.
27. Peter Kingsford, **The Hunger Marchers in Britain 1920-1940**, London 1982, p. 157.
28. In Belfast, 'Fighting with the police reached such proportions that the Royal Inniskillen Fusiliers equipped with machine guns were drafted into the city, martial law was imposed and the troops fired on the workers killing two and wounding scores.' Gorman, op cit., p. 144.
29. Peter Hain, **Political Strikes, the State and Trade Unionism in Britain**, Harmondsworth 1986, p. 37.
30. Bunyan, op cit., p. 70.
31. Judge and Reynolds, op cit., p. 236.
32. Critchley, op cit., p. 250.
33. Report of HM Inspector of Constabulary, **PP 1950 XIII**, p. 30.
34. Critchley, op cit., p. 238.
35. 'Evidence of Police Federation', para. 11, 'Royal Commission on Police Interim Report of Chairman Willick', **PP 1960/61**.
36. **PP 1961/62 XX**.
37. Judge and Reynolds, op cit., p. 238.
38. Ibid. gives rise as 40 to 50 percent.
39. Whittaker, op cit., p. 58.
40. Ibid., p. 58.
41. **Guardian**, 22 August 1980.
42. Quoted in Hain, op cit., p. 184.
43. Roger Graef, **Talking Blues. The Police in Their Own Words**,

London 1989, p. 120.

44. Leon Trotsky, **The Struggle Against Fascism in Germany**, New York 1971, p. 147.

6. Post war

References for police strength between 1948 and 1990, unless otherwise stated have been taken for this chapter from HM Inspector of Constabulary Reports for the appropriate years to be found in the following Parliamentary Papers:

PP 1987/88 XXXIX HC, p. 521; **PP 1987/88 VIII HC**, p. 32; **PP 1987/88 CM**, p. 32; **PP 1985/86 XXXVII CM**, p. 437; **PP 1984/85 XLIV HC**, p. 469; **PP 1983/84 XLII CM**, p. 528; **PP 1983/84 VII HC**, p. 15; **PP 1981/82 XLIV HC**, p. 463; **PP 1980/81 XXXV HC**, p. 409; **PP 1979/80 XLV**, p. 725; **PP 1979/80 XII**, p. 135; **PP 1977/78 XLVI**, p. 545; **PP 1976/77 XXXIX**, p. 414; **PP 1975/76 XXXIX**, p. 6496; **PP 1974/75 XXX**, p. 406; **PP 1974 XIV**, p. 145; **PP 1972/73 XXVIII**, p. 289; **PP 1971/72 XXXIII**, p. 290; **PP 1970/71 XLIII**, p. 4680; **PP 1969/70 XXIV**, p. 308; **PP 1968/69 XLIV**, p. 305; **PP 1967/68 XXX**, p. 272; **PP 1966/67 XLVI**, p. 544; **PP 1966/67 XLVI**, p. 90; **PP 1964/65 XXI**, p. 251; **PP 1963/64 XVIII**, p. 259; **PP 1962/63 XXIII**, p. 250; **PP 1961/62 XX**, p. 220; **PP 1960/61 XX**, p. 337; **PP 1959/60 XX**, p. 257; **PP 1958/59 XVIII**, p. 202; **PP 1957/58 XVII**, p. 218; **PP 1956/57 XVIII**, p. 210; **PP 1955/56 XXVI**, p. 203; **PP 1954/55 VII**, p. 50; **PP 1953/54 XVIII**, p. 161; **PP 1952/53 XVI**, p. 216; **BPP 1951/52 XVII**, p. 208; **PP 1950/51 XVIII**, p. 194; **PP 1950 XIII**, p. 90; **PP 1948/49 XIX**, p. 160; **PP 1947/48 XIV**, p. 143.

1. Hal Draper, **Karl Marx's Theory of Revolution**, vol. 1, 'State and Bureaucracy', New York 1977, p. 291.
2. Ibid., p. 251.
3. John Moylan, **The Police in Britain**, p. 12.
4. Steve Peak, **Troops in Strikes. Military Intervention in Industrial Disputes**, London 1984, p. 83.
5. Ibid., pp. 11-12.
6. 'Report of the Metropolitan Commissioner of Police for the year 1959', p. 15, **PP 1959/60 XX**. My emphasis.
7. 'Statistics from Inspector of Constabulary Reports', **PP 1954/55 VII**, p. 31; **PP1960/61 XX**, p. 29.
8. 'Metropolitan Commissioners Report', **PP 1959/60**, p. 16.
9. Calculated from **Reports of the Commissioner of Police of the Metropolis** for 1964 and 1970. For the use of MI5 against workers see Tony Cliff and Donny Gluckstein, **The Labour Party: A Marxist History**, London 1988, p. 288.

10. **Policing**, vol. 3, London Summer 1987, p. 97.
11. Table 13. Civilians employed by the police.

Year	Whole time	Year	Whole time	Part time
1948	4,533	1970	23,321	
1950	4,203	1972	26,642	
1952	4,722	1974	29,554	
1954	6,128	1976	30,628	7,846
1956	6,976	1978	30,976	7,322
1958	7,503	1980	33,537	8,355
1960	8,446	1982	33,738	7,832
1962	9,917	1984	35,232	7,331
1964	11,430	1986	37,152	6,231
1966	15,056	1988	39,209	6,212
1968	19,818	1990	42,715	6,511

The figures for part timers were not given before 1976 but it was indicated in 1970 that part time equivalents were contained within the full time number. The figures for civilians employed by the Metropolitan and City police are included, but not those employed by the Receiver of the Metropolitan Police. In 1948 there were 646 men, 3,146 women and 741 youths. When the division between men and women was included, women vastly outnumbered men. The classification was then changed to civilian technical and domestic.

12. Table 14. Traffic wardens and police.

Year	Police	Traffic wardens	Year	Police	Traffic wardens
1967	91,043	4,192	1979	113,309	4,275
1968	91,172	4,121	1980	117,423	4,296
1969	92,262	4,468	1981	119,575	4,455
1970	94,312	5,043	1982	120,951	4,597
1971	97,326	5,840	1983	121,003	4,914
1972	100,009	6,356	1984	120,573	4,860
1973	100,910	6,231	1985	120,702	4,769
1974	102,467	5,943	1986	121,550	4,793
1975	107,138	6,193	1987	124,102	4,754
1976	109,476	5,867	1988	124,759	4,644
1977	-	-	1989	126,110	4,604
1978	109,075	4,678	1990	127,090	4,808

Figures taken from police reports and are of total police strength including women, Metropolitan and City police. Traffic warden figures include senior traffic wardens.

13. Chanie Rosenberg, **1919, Britain on the Brink of Revolution**, London 1987, p. 24.
14. Nor are flying pickets peculiar to Britain in the twentieth century. During the Somerset coal miners' strike in the US in 1922-23 it was said, 'for a hundred years, it has been a habit of strikers to start marches through nearby towns that might join.' Blankenhorn, **Strike for Union**, New York 1924, p. 59.
15. Michael Crick, **Scargill and the Miners**, Harmondsworth 1985, p. 60.
16. Quoted in Keith Jeffrey and Peter Hennessy, **States of Emergency**, London 1983, p. 235.
17. Ibid., p. 236.
18. Peak, op cit., p. 123.
19. Roger Geary, **Policing Industrial Disputes 1893-1985**, London 1985, p. 88.
20. Peak, op cit., p. 75.
21. Mark Dickinson, **To Break a Union**, Manchester 1984, p. 136.
22. **Financial Times**, 1 December 1983.
23. **Guardian**, 10 October 1984.
24. Liz Curtis, **They Shoot Children**, London 1982, p. 11.
25. James Cramer, **The World's Police**, London 1964, p. 215.
26. BSSRS, **Techno Cop**, London 1985, p. 79.
27. Ibid., p. 78.
28. Ibid., p. 79.
29. Geary, op cit., p. 114.
30. See Gerry Northam, **Shooting in the Dark. Riot Police in Britain**, London 1988.
31. Centre for Research on Criminal Justice, **Iron Fist and Velvet Glove**, Berkeley 1975, p. 74.
32. **Sunday Times**, 12 December 1983.
33. Curtis, op cit., p. 11.
34. BSSRS, op cit., p. 71.
35. Ibid., p. 74.
36. Curtis, op cit., p. 6.
37. **Guardian**, 16 July 1981.
38. Quoted in **New Society**, 2 August 1984.
39. Geary, op cit., p. 18.
40. See Michael Zander, **The Police and Criminal Evidence Act 1984**, London 1985.
41. 'Getting away with it', **Socialist Review**, London 1980:15.
42. **Report of the Commissioner of Police of the Metropolis 1986**, CM 158, London 1987, pp. 37, 42, 137.

43. Draper, op cit., p. 292.
44. **Financial Times,** 25 May 1989.

7. Police and the right

1. Quoted in Frederick Mullaly, 'Fascism inside England', in Stewart Bowes, ed., **The Police and Civil Liberties,** London 1966, p. 46.
2. Ibid., p. 52.
3. Kenneth Sloane, **Law and Disorder,** (**Police Review** publication), London 1978, pp. 7-8.
4. John Rees, 'What Intelligence?', **Socialist Worker Review,** London January 1987.
5. Ibid.
6. **Sunday Times,** 23 January 1983.
7. Rees, op cit.
8. **Guardian,** 13 October 1986.
9. Lobster, **MI5 and the Rise of Thatcher. Covert Operations in British Politics 1974-1978.**
10. **Sunday Times,** 1 November 1985.
11. **Guardian,** 21 November 1986.
12. James Rusbridger, **The Intelligence Game,** London 1989, p. 160.
13. Ibid., p. 159.
14. **Guardian,** 10 March 1985.
15. Rusbridger, op cit., p. 171.
16. Chapman Pincher, **Their Trade is Treachery,** London 1981, p. 78.
17. See Paul Foot, **Who Framed Colin Wallace?,** London 1990.
18. Tony Bunyan, **The History and Practice of the Political Police in Britain,** London 1987, p. 104.
19. Quoted in Ibid., p. 123.
20. Rusbridger, op cit., p. 161.
21. Ibid., p. 162.
22. Ibid., p. 170.
23. Ibid., p. 162.
24. **Guardian,** 11 May 1985.
25. BSSRS, **Techno Cop,** London 1985, p. 31.
26. Bunyan, op cit., p. 138.
27. Ibid.
28. BSSRS, op cit., p. 34.
29. Rusbridger, op cit., p. 159.
30. Tom Bowden, **Beyond the Limits of the Law,** pp. 253-4.
31. Ibid., p. 254.
32. Ibid., p. 257.
33. Ibid., p. 258.

34. Mark Hollingsworth and Charles Tremayne, **The Economic League: the Silent McCarthyism**, London 1989, p. iv.
35. Ibid., p. 1.
36. Ibid., pp. 5-6. Hall was one of the conspirators who produced the forged Zinoviev letter in 1924 about an alleged Communist plot.
37. Ibid., p. 21.
38. Ibid.
39. Ibid., p. 71.
40. Ibid., p. 34.
41. Ibid., pp. 82, 107.
42. Ibid., p. 20.

8. Racism

1. **Guardian**, 25 May 1984.
2. Phil Scraton, **Law and Order and the Authoritarian State**, Buckingham 1987, p. 172.
3. **Race and Immigration**, no. 207, London September 1987.
4. Peter Fryer, **Black People in the British Empire**, London 1988, p. 122.
5. David J Smith and Jeremy Gray, **Police and People in London**, vol. 4, Policy Study Insititute, no. 621, London 1983, p. 123.
6. Ibid., p. 33.
7. Ibid., p. 116.
8. Ibid.
9. Lord Scarman, **Scarman Report** (Pelican edition), London 1986, p. xvii.
10. National Convention of Black Teachers, **Police Racism and Union Collusion. The John Fernandes Case**, pp. 2-5.
11. Robert Reiner, **The Politics of the Police**, Brighton 1985, p. 102.
12. Smith and Gray, op cit., p. 113.
13. **Racial Attacks and Harassment**, Home Affairs Committee HC 17, London 1989, p. ix.
14. Ibid.
15. Ibid., p. xi.
16. **Guardian**, 31 October 1990.
17. **Racial Attacks and Harassment**, op cit., p. 33.
18. **Race, Crime and Arrests**. Home Office Research Studies no. 58, London 1979. p. 33.
19. David J Smith, **Police and People in London**, vol. 3. Policy Studies Institute no. 620, London 1983, p. 100.
20. Ibid, p. 129.
21. **Race and Immigration**, London, May 1990.

22. **Guardian**, 24 August 1982.
23. Smith and Gray, op cit., p. 118.
24. **Guardian**, 3 February 1981.
25. **Racial Attacks and Harassment**, op cit., p. iv.
26. Fryer, op cit., p. 125.
27. Ibid., p. 124.
28. Ibid., p. 125.
29. **Guardian**, 25 May 1981.
30. Fryer, op cit., p. 123.
31. Ibid.; **Race and Immigration**, no. 235, London May 1990; Ibid., no. 227, July/August 1989; Ibid., no. 232, February 1990.
32. There has always been some offence on the British statute book for which the police required no warrant to conduct raids.
33. Early dates from, **Police Against Black People**, Race and Class pamphlet no. 6, evidence submitted to the Royal Commission on Criminal Procedure by the Institute of Race Relations, London 1979, p. 9.
34. **Race and Immigration**, no. 227, London March 1981.
35. **Financial Times**, 28 January 1980.
36. **Guardian**, 24 June 1986.
37. Smith and Gray, op cit., p. 130.
38. **Sunday Times**, 16 August 1981.
39. Chris Harman, 'The riots of 1981', **International Socialism**, 2:14, Lodnon 1981, p. 14.
40. Table 15. Number of times stopped by the police in the past twelve months: men by age and ethnic group, in vehicle or on foot.

	White			West Indian			Asian		
Age	15-24	25-44	45+	15-24	25-44	45+	15-24	25-44	45+
% stopped	44	28	10	63	36	12	18	9	4
Ave. no. of stops among those stopped.	2.58	1.59	1.25	4.10	1.77	1.57	2.09	1.35	1.00

David J Smith, **Police and People in London**, vol. 1, Policy Studies Institute no. 618, London 1983, p. 100.

It can be seen that although the police pick on those they classify as West Indian it is also the case that white youths come in for more police harassment than do middle age West Indians or Asians.
41. **Guardian**, 19 September 1981.
42. In 1983 this sentiment was expressed by a London police officer: 'I don't mind them being nosey. After all, they pay our wages, the ratepayers and property owners.' Smith and Gray, op cit., p. 73.

43. Carolyn Steadman, **Policing the Victorian Community**, London 1984, p. 57.
44. Royden Harrison, **Before the Socialists**, London 1965, p. 117.
45. Superintendent John Robinson, **Catching Criminals**, (published by **Police Review**), London 1978, p. 27.
46. Ibid., p. 23.
47. **Guardian**, 21 June 1982.
48. Smith, op cit., p. 267.
49. Maurice Punch, **Policing the Inner City, a Study of Amsterdam's Warmoesstraat**, London 1979, pp. 175-6.

9. Family and sex

1. Eric Hobsbawm, **Industry and Empire**, Harmondsworth 1968, p. 159.
2. Judith Walkowitz, **Prostitution and Victorian Society**, Cambridge 1980, p. 71.
3. Ibid., p. 2.
4. Ibid., p. 175.
5. There was a similar exercise of police powers in Poland. A decree of the Warsaw chief of police forced women factory workers and prostitutes to suffer humiliating medical examinations. The Polish revolutionary socialist party led a successful struggle against this in 1883. In a weaving mill at Zyrad 6,000 workers struck. The strike was bloodily suppressed; but the decree had to be withdrawn. See Paul Frolich, **Rosa Luxemburg**, London 1972.
6. WW Sanger, **The History of Prostitution**, New York 1917, p. 141.
7. **Yorkshire Evening Post**, 3 May 1982.
8. Claude Jaget, ed., **Prostitutes: Our Life**, Bristol 1980, p. 15.
9. Ibid.
10. Ibid., p. 30.
11. Ibid., p. 41.
12. Pamela Roby, 'Revision of the New York State Penal Law on Prostitution', **Social Problems**, 17, Massachusetts 1969-1970, p. 97.
13. **Guardian**, 13 April 1988.
14. 'Prostitution', BBC 2, 22 February 1988.
15. Walkowitz, op cit., p. 256.
16. Ibid.
17. Noel Halifax, **Gay Liberation and the Struggle for Socialism**, London 1988, p. 10.
18. **Times**, 26 March 1982.

19. Paul Crane, **Gays and the Law**, London n.d., p. 40.
20. **Guardian**, 25 January 1987.
21. **Socialist Worker**, 16 February 1991.
22. Joan Locke, **The British Police Woman**, London 1979, p. 28.
23. Ibid., p. 48.
24. 'Committee on the Employment of Women on Police Duties 1920 (Baird Committee) Minutes of Evidence', CMD 113, **PP 1921 XVI**, London 1921, p. 21.
25. 'Report of the Commissioner of Police of the Metropolis 1918 and 1919', **PP 1920 XXII**, p. 501; 'Report of the Commissioner of Police of the Metropolis 1921', **PP 1922 X**, p. 42.
26. Mariensson, **Crime and the Police**, Harmondsworth 1953, p. 197.
27. David J Smith and Jeremy Gray, **Police and People in London**, vol. 4, Policy Studies Institute, no. 621, Lndon 1983, p. 91.
28. **Guardian**, 12 April 1985.
29. BBC1, 19 January 1982.
30. Quoted in Grimstad, Kirsten and Renni, **The New Woman's Survival Catalogue**, New York 1973.
31. Quoted in **Rape Controversy**, NCCL Report 23; Ian Blair, 'Investigating Rape', **Times**, 25 January 1985.
32. **Guardian**, 15 January 1992.
33. See Barry Cox, John Shirley and Martin Short, **The Fall of Scotland Yard**, Harmondsworth 1977, p. 154.
34. Celia Petty, Deborah Roberts and Sharon Smith, **Women's Liberation and Socialism**, Chicago 1987, p. 70.
35. Ibid., p. 71.
36. **Guardian**, 10 February 1987.
37. Locke, op cit., p. 192.

10. Sport and the Kop

1. Leon Radzinowicz, **A History of Criminal Law**, vol. 3, London 1956, p. 234.
2. Ibid., p. 266.
3. Ibid.
4. Ibid., p. 19.
5. Ibid., p. 275.
6. Ibid., pp. 18.
7. Ibid., pp. 18-19.
8. Robert Storch, 'The Plague of Blue Locusts', in Mike Fitzgerald, Gregor McLennan and Jennie Pawson, eds., **Crime and Society**, London 1981, p. 103.

9. George Dilnot, **The Story of Scotland Yard**, London n.d., p. 329.
10. Critchley, **A History of Police in England and Wales 900-1966**, London 1967, p. 147.
11. David J Smith and Jeremy Gray, **Police and People in London**, vol 4, Policy Studies Institute no. 621, London 1983, p. 83.
12. Storch, op cit., p. 105.
13. **Guardian**, 20 August 1985.
14. Storch, op cit., p. 104.
15. Stephen Humphries, **Hooligans or Rebels?**, Oxford 1981, p. 149.
16. Geoffrey Pearson, **Hooligan. A History of Respectable Fears**, Basingstoke 1983, p. 66.
17. Ibid., p. 67.
18. Ibid., p. 68.
19. Humphries, op cit., p. 207.
20. Ibid., p. 203.
21. Phil Cohen, 'Policing the Working Class City', in Fitzgerald et al., op cit., p. 118.
22. John English and Robert Houghton, **Summonses and Charges**, revised edition, London 1980, p. 145.
23. Pearson, op cit., p. 108.
24. Ibid., p. 71.
25. Ibid., p. 65.
26. **Guardian**, 13 April 1987.
27. Pearson, op cit., p. 64. Rivalry between supporters predates capitalism. 'There are truly astonishing similarities between football rowdyism and the violent disputes between hostile factions at theatres and hippodromes ... more than a thousand years ago... Blues and Greens chanted their support for rival champions in chariot races, each faction grouped at opposing "ends" of the stadiums.' Ibid., p. 221.
28. See Simon Inglis, **The Football Grounds of England and Wales**, London 1985, pp. 29-36, 268; May, **World Soccer**, 1989, p. 5; **Socialist Worker**, 22 April 1989; **The Star**, April 18 1989.
29. **Sunday Times**, 18 August 1985.
30. **Guardian**, 6 June 1985.
31. Ibid., 22 July 1986.
32. Inglis, op cit., p. 32.
33. **Shoot**, 25 July 1985.
34. Ibid.
35. **Socialist Worker**, 22 April 1989.
36. **Guardian**, 18 April 1989.
37. **The Star**, 18 April 1989.
38. **Daily Express**, 18 April 1989.
39. 'Hard News', Channel Four, 2 November 1990.
40. Taped Interview with Robert Kincaid.

41. 'Report of the Commissioner of the Metropolitan Police', **PP 1956/57 XVIII**, p. 29.

11. The problem redefined

1. Dennis Chapman, **Sociology and the Stereotype of the Criminal**, London 1968, p. 55.
2. Simon Fields, **Trends in Crime and their Interpretation. A Study of Recorded Crime in Post War England and Wales**. Home Office Research Study 119, London 1990. p. 5.
3. Ibid., p. 20.
4. Ibid., p. 49.
5. Chapman, op cit., p. 75.
6. David J Smith **Police and People in London**, vol. 1, Policy Studies Institute no. 618, London 1983, pp. 10, 12.
7. **Guardian**, 9 July 1983.
8. Ibid.
9. **Criminal Statistics England and Wales 1988**, CM 847, London 1989, p. 107.
10. **Report of the Commissioner of Police of the Metropolis 1986**, CM 158, London 1987, p. 79.
11. **Guardian**, 13 November 1981.
12. Ibid., 15 February 1983.
13. **Report of the Commissioner of Police of the Metropolis 1989**, CM 1070, London 1990, p. 120.
14. Fields, op cit., p. 9.
15. **A new package of policies from Labour: People First,** London 1986.
16. In my workplace security officers employed to stop crime were used by management to take down anti Gulf War posters and get rid of 'outsiders' leafletting for meetings against the Gulf War in the college canteen.
17. Quoted in **Protecting our People**, Labour Party policy document, London 1987, p. 18.
18. **Labour's Programme 1982**, London 1982, p. 179.
19. Barry Loveday, **The Role and Effectiveness of the Merseyside Police Committee**, a report commissioned by Merseyside County Council, Birmingham 1985, p. 127.
20. Ibid., p. 169.
21. **Guardian**, 11 August 1984.
22. Steve Peak, **Troops in Strikes**, Cobden Trust 1984, p. 158.
23. Keith Jeffrey and Peter Hennessy, **States of Emergency**, London 1983, p. 237.

24. Robert Mark, **In the Office of Constable**, London 1979, p. 160.
25. **Protecting our People**, op cit., p. 13.
26. Roger Geary, **Policing Industrial Disputes 1893-1985**, London 1985, p. 70.
27. Ibid., pp. 87, 88.
28. Tony Cliff and Donny Gluckstein, **The Labour Party: a Marxist History**, London 1988, p. 341.
29. Loveday, op cit., p. 174.
30. **Guardian**, 23 July 1984.
31. Ibid., 4 October 1984.
32. Cliff and Gluckstein, op cit., p. 50.
33. **Guardian**, 27 January 1987.
34. **Protecting our People**, op cit., p. 14. A Labour government passed the Prevention of Terrorism Act in 1974. Under the Act between 1974 and 1986 6,000 were arrested and only 17 actually charged with terrorist offences: Tony Bunyan, **The Political Police in Britain**, London 1977, p. 54. Labour was also responsible for the 1968 Immigration Act.
35. **Guardian**, 14 January 1981.
36. Crispin Aubrey, **Who's Watching You?**, Harmondsworth 1981, p. 36.
37. **Guardian**, 23 January 1987.
38. Neil Kinnock's speech to the 1985 Labour Party conference.
39. **Protecting our People**, op cit., pp. 3-5.
40. Robert Reiner, **The Politics of the Police**, Brighton 1985, p. 54.
41. Robert Baldwin and Richard Kinsey, **Police Powers and Politics**, London 1982, p. 224.
42. Gill Hubbard, unpublished research paper, 'A Critique of Community Policing'.
43. Baldwin and Kinsey, op cit., p. 224.
44. Hubbard, op cit.
45. **Guardian**, 3 September 1981.
46. Ibid.
47. 'General Instructions to the Metropolitan Police 1829', quoted in Baldwin and Kinsey, op cit., p. 26.
48. Ibid., p. 224.
49. Loveday, op cit., p. 105.
50. **Sunday Times**, 17 January 1982.
51. Smith, op cit., pp. 299-300.
52. Phil Scraton, **Law and Order and the Authoritarian State**, Buckingham 1987, p. 102.
53. Lord Scarman, **The Scarman Report** (Pelican edition), London 1986, p. xvi.
54. Reiner, op cit., p. 210.
55. BSSRS, **Techno Cop**, London 1985, p. 108.

Conclusion

1. See p. 27.
2. **Report of the Commissioner of Police of the Metropolis 1986**, Cm 158, London 1987, p. 137.
3. Pierre Broué and Emile Termine, **The Revolution and Civil War in Spain**, London 1972, p. 122.
4. George Orwell, **Homage to Catalonia**, London 1971, p. 2.
5. Karl Marx and Frederick Engels, **The Civil War in France**, in id., **Selected Works**, vol. 1, Moscow 1955, p. 529.
6. Eamonn McCann, **War and an Irish Town**, London 1980, p. 100.
7. Engels, 'Origin of the Family, Private Property and the State', **Marx and Engels Selected Works**, Moscow 1970, p. 581.

Index

Other publications from Bookmarks

The Changing Working Class / *Alex Callinicos and Chris Harman*
> Capitalism continually revolutionises production, and does the same to the working class. Does this mean today's white collar workers are really middle class? Has the traditional manual working class disappeared? Is the workforce now split between a core and periphery? *£3.50 / $6.75*

Racism, Resistance and Revolution / *Peter Alexander*
> Many millions of people abhor racism, but where does it come from, and how can it be fought? This book brings together decades of anti racist experience to argue for an effective strategy. *£3.95 / $7.50*

1919: Britain on the Brink of Revolution / *Chanie Rosenberg*
> In 1919 the prime minister told trade union leaders: 'in our opinion we are at your mercy'. This book draws on cabinet records to consider how close Britain came to revolution in 1919, and what forces prevented it. *£2.25 / $4.50*

Marxism and the Trade Union Struggle: the General Strike of 1926 / *Tony Cliff and Donny Gluckstein*
> An analysis of the dymanics, strengths and limitations of trade union organisation. This book centres on the General Strike of 1926, but contains valuable insights for trade unionism everywhere. *£6.95 / $11.95*

All available from good bookshops, or by post from Bookmarks
(add 10 percent postage)
Bookmarks
265 Seven Sisters Road, London N4 2DE, England
PO Box 16085, Chicago, Il. 60616, US
GPO Box 1473N, Melbourne 3001, Australia